MW01041755

Set Your Day: A 365 day gratitude journal

Published by Heather K. Lopez

ISBN 978-1-6780-7767-9

Introduction

Gratitude is one of the most vital emotions that can fulfill our minds and hearts in order to create extraordinary opportunities. When someone is filled with gratitude you can not only see it, you can feel it bouncing off of them and it is highly contagious. Almost like that same warm feeling when you are standing in the sun. This book's main focus is gratitude with some additions that will help your affirmations become much more meaningful and achievable. Oh, and a spot for doodling! Who doesn't appreciate the occasional doodle?

You will notice the inspirational quotes located at the bottom of each page. All of these quotes come from individuals who live or once lived in my local community in Upstate NY. My husband and I are huge fans of being fully involved in and giving back to our community. Your community is only as good as you make it. Mahatma Gandhi said "*Be the change you wish to see in the world*". I truly believe that, like this amazing visionary, we should all aspire to be that change which will act as the catalyst to ignite others around us.

This book was one of my goals for 2021. 2020 was one of the most difficult years for many people across the world. My husband and I are both in healthcare and as you can imagine, exhausted to the point that we never thought we could bear. This was the first pandemic we have experienced and it certainly tried not only us but our careers, friendships, family and community. I thought to myself, "I am going to develop a tool that will inspire others to set their day up for success." And here it is! I hope you have fun throughout your journey and that this book helps you become more comfortable expressing yourself through gratitude.

I am an only child to Frank and Susan Casler and they have always instilled in me that if you want something, the only person to make it happen is you. I am blessed to have been provided with 2 amazing parents that ingrained the meaning of determination from a young age. So with this book, I am doing just that, making it happen. I now pass the torch to you to make it happen in your own life! *You Got This*, 365 days ahead!

Much love, H

January **1**, *20____*

Today's Doodle

National Bloody Mary Day

3 Tasks for the day

- ❑ _____
- ❑ _____
- ❑ _____

Gratitude Reflection- What is one thing that you are thankful for today?

_____
_____
_____
_____
_____

January **2**, *20____*

Today's Doodle

National Science Fiction Day

3 Tasks for the day

- ❑ _____
- ❑ _____
- ❑ _____

Gratitude Reflection- What is one thing that you are thankful for today?

_____
_____
_____
_____
_____

Gratitude gives you so much more opportunity in your day than you could ever imagine!

HKL- Hagaman NY

January **3**, 20____   *Today's Doodle*

National Chocolate Covered Cherry Day

3 Tasks for the day

- ❑ _____
- ❑ _____
- ❑ _____

Gratitude Reflection- What is one thing that you are thankful for today?

_____
_____
_____
_____
_____

January **4**, 20____   *Today's Doodle*

National Trivia Day

3 Tasks for the day

- ❑ _____
- ❑ _____
- ❑ _____

Gratitude Reflection- What is one thing that you are thankful for today?

_____
_____
_____
_____
_____

Forsake time to cry; to make time to try; then take time to fly.
Sue Blazejewski- Amsterdam NY

January **5**, 20____

National Whipped Cream Day

3 Tasks for the day

- ❑ _____
- ❑ _____
- ❑ _____

Today's Doodle

Gratitude Reflection- What is one thing that you are thankful for today?

_____
_____
_____
_____
_____

January **6**, 20____

National Technology Day

3 Tasks for the day

- ❑ _____
- ❑ _____
- ❑ _____

Today's Doodle

Gratitude Reflection- What is one thing that you are thankful for today?

_____
_____
_____
_____
_____

Blooms can weather any storm because of the roots binding strength, bond and courage! Michelle Wetsky- Amsterdam NY

January **7**, 20___

National Tempura Day

3 Tasks for the day

- ☐ _____
- ☐ _____
- ☐ _____

Today's Doodle

Gratitude Reflection- What is one thing that you are thankful for today?

_____
_____
_____
_____
_____

January **8**, 20___

National Bubble Bath Day

3 Tasks for the day

- ☐ _____
- ☐ _____
- ☐ _____

Today's Doodle

Gratitude Reflection- What is one thing that you are thankful for today?

_____
_____
_____
_____
_____

The struggle of 3 engagements everyday: #1 re-engage and power through a conversation with someone who you had a negative experience with #2 engage win conversations with someone new #3 engage with a new experience based on advice from listening to others.
Ginger Champain- Amsterdam NY

January **9**, 20____

National Apricot Day

3 Tasks for the day

- ❑ _____
- ❑ _____
- ❑ _____

Gratitude Reflection- What is one thing that you are thankful for today?

_____
_____
_____
_____
_____

January **10**, 20____   Today's Doodle

National Save The Eagles Day

3 Tasks for the day

- ❑ _____
- ❑ _____
- ❑ _____

Gratitude Reflection- What is one thing that you are thankful for today?

_____
_____
_____
_____
_____

Take a chance at life, you never know how much time you have. No what ifs and no regrets.
Priscilla Rogers- Amsterdam NY

January **11**, *20____*   *Today's Doodle*

National Milk Day

3 Tasks for the day

- ❏ _____
- ❏ _____
- ❏ _____

Gratitude Reflection- What is one thing that you are thankful for today?

_____
_____
_____
_____
_____

January **12**, *20____*   *Today's Doodle*

National Curried Chicken Day

3 Tasks for the day

- ❏ _____
- ❏ _____
- ❏ _____

Gratitude Reflection- What is one thing that you are thankful for today?

_____
_____
_____
_____
_____

The book of life never has to end, just keep adding new chapters and make it what you want.
Kim Martin- Rotterdam NY

January **13**, 20____

National Sticker Day

3 Tasks for the day

- ❏ _____
- ❏ _____
- ❏ _____

Today's Doodle

Gratitude Reflection- What is one thing that you are thankful for today?

_____
_____
_____
_____
_____

January **14**, 20____

National Dress Up Your Pet Day

3 Tasks for the day

- ❏ _____
- ❏ _____
- ❏ _____

Today's Doodle

Gratitude Reflection- What is one thing that you are thankful for today?

_____
_____
_____
_____
_____

Smile, it'll make people wonder what you're up to. Gina DeRossi- Amsterdam NY

January **15**, *20____*

National Bagel Day

3 Tasks for the day

    ❏ _____
    ❏ _____
    ❏ _____

Today's Doodle

Gratitude Reflection- What is one thing that you are thankful for today?

_____
_____
_____
_____
_____

January **16**, *20____*

National Fig Newton Day

3 Tasks for the day

    ❏ _____
    ❏ _____
    ❏ _____

Today's Doodle

Gratitude Reflection- What is one thing that you are thankful for today?

_____
_____
_____
_____
_____

Believe in yourself, never stop learning and always stay humble.
Chrissy Przybylowicz- Amsterdam NY

January **17**, 20____

Today's Doodle

National Hot Buttered Rum Day

3 Tasks for the day

- ❑ _____
- ❑ _____
- ❑ _____

Gratitude Reflection- What is one thing that you are thankful for today?

_____
_____
_____
_____
_____

January **18**, 20____

Today's Doodle

National Winnie The Pooh Day

3 Tasks for the day

- ❑ _____
- ❑ _____
- ❑ _____

Gratitude Reflection- What is one thing that you are thankful for today?

_____
_____
_____
_____
_____

When life is difficult and painful, remember to keep moving forward, learning, adapting and evolving. By staying focused on the goal it may appear you have magical thinking and will it to be.
Liz Peterson- Fultonville NY

January **19**, *20____*

National Popcorn Day

3 Tasks for the day

    ❑ _____
    ❑ _____
    ❑ _____

Gratitude Reflection- What is one thing that you are thankful for today?

_____
_____
_____
_____
_____

Today's Doodle

January **20**, *20____*

National Cheese Lover's Day

3 Tasks for the day

    ❑ _____
    ❑ _____
    ❑ _____

Gratitude Reflection- What is one thing that you are thankful for today?

_____
_____
_____
_____
_____

Today's Doodle

Have intense trust that no matter what happens, you have what it takes to respond powerfully to whatever happens.
Todd Cetnar- Mental Performance Coach- Saratoga Springs NY

January **21**, *20____*

National Hugging Day

3 Tasks for the day

❑ _____
❑ _____
❑ _____

Today's Doodle

Gratitude Reflection- What is one thing that you are thankful for today?

_____
_____
_____
_____
_____

January **22**, *20____*

National Blonde Brownie Day

3 Tasks for the day

❑ _____
❑ _____
❑ _____

Today's Doodle

Gratitude Reflection- What is one thing that you are thankful for today?

_____
_____
_____
_____
_____

When you are filled with gratitude; everyone around you can feel and see it, that is not a bad thing!
HKL- Hagaman NY

January **23,** *20____*

National Pie Day

Today's Doodle

3 Tasks for the day

❑ _____
❑ _____
❑ _____

Gratitude Reflection- What is one thing that you are thankful for today?

_____
_____
_____
_____
_____

January **24,** *20____*

National Compliment Day

Today's Doodle

3 Tasks for the day

❑ _____
❑ _____
❑ _____

Gratitude Reflection- What is one thing that you are thankful for today?

_____
_____
_____
_____
_____

Time, the most precious created gift anyone can give you. GL- Hagaman NY

January **25**, *20____*

National Irish Coffee Day

3 Tasks for the day

- ❑ _____
- ❑ _____
- ❑ _____

Gratitude Reflection- What is one thing that you are thankful for today?

_____
_____
_____
_____
_____

January **26**, *20____*

Today's Doodle

National Spouses Day

3 Tasks for the day

- ❑ _____
- ❑ _____
- ❑ _____

Gratitude Reflection- What is one thing that you are thankful for today?

_____
_____
_____
_____
_____

You have to want to get stronger; you have to want to change and grow.
Robert D. Morris- Amsterdam NY

January **27**, *20____*   *Today's Doodle*

National Chocolate Cake Day

3 Tasks for the day

- ❑ _____
- ❑ _____
- ❑ _____

Gratitude Reflection- What is one thing that you are thankful for today?

_____
_____
_____
_____
_____

January **28**, *20____*   *Today's Doodle*

National Data Privacy Day

3 Tasks for the day

- ❑ _____
- ❑ _____
- ❑ _____

Gratitude Reflection- What is one thing that you are thankful for today?

_____
_____
_____
_____
_____

Always strive to be a human being rather than a human doing. Susan Casler- Glenn NY

January **29**, 20____

Today's Doodle

National Corn Chip Day

3 Tasks for the day

❑ _____
❑ _____
❑ _____

Gratitude Reflection- What is one thing that you are thankful for today?

_____
_____
_____
_____
_____

January **30**, 20____

Today's Doodle

National Croissant Day

3 Tasks for the day

❑ _____
❑ _____
❑ _____

Gratitude Reflection- What is one thing that you are thankful for today?

_____
_____
_____
_____
_____

It is important to not only dream of success but to wake up each morning and work hard to achieve those very same dreams! - be innovative, immagnitive, focused and enthusiastic about the adventures that lie ahead- be confident in your ability to perform in an exemplary fashion and to contribute with distinction! Dr. Hardies- Amsterdam NY

January **31**, *20____*   *Today's Doodle*

National Inspire Your Heart With Art Day

3 Tasks for the day

❑ _____
❑ _____
❑ _____

Gratitude Reflection- What is one thing that you are thankful for today?

_____
_____
_____
_____
_____

February **1**, *20____*   *Today's Doodle*

National Get Up Day

3 Tasks for the day

❑ _____
❑ _____
❑ _____

Gratitude Reflection- What is one thing that you are thankful for today?

_____
_____
_____
_____
_____

I believe we should live our lives in such a way that we look back and say.... That was a great day, a great week, a great month, a great year. Go out and make some memories.
Andy Heck- Amsterdam N

February **2**, 20___

National Groundhog Day

3 Tasks for the day

❑ _____
❑ _____
❑ _____

Today's Doodle

Gratitude Reflection- What is one thing that you are thankful for today?

_____
_____
_____
_____

February **3**, 20___

National Carrot Cake Day

3 Tasks for the day

❑ _____
❑ _____
❑ _____

Today's Doodle

Gratitude Reflection- What is one thing that you are thankful for today?

_____
_____
_____
_____
_____

It's not simply what you say that counts, but you must understand how people will take it.
Victor Giulianelli - Amsterdam NY

February **4**, 20____

National Optimist Day

3 Tasks for the day

- ❑ _____
- ❑ _____
- ❑ _____

Today's Doodle

Gratitude Reflection- What is one thing that you are thankful for today?

_____
_____
_____
_____
_____

February **5**, 20____

World Nutella Day

3 Tasks for the day

- ❑ _____
- ❑ _____
- ❑ _____

Today's Doodle

Gratitude Reflection- What is one thing that you are thankful for today?

_____
_____
_____
_____
_____

In life everyone will endure misfortunes and agony. We must continue to persevere with
hope and strength in our mind and hearts, because only we can create our own
opportunities.   A. Spagnola LPN- Johnstown NY

February **6**, 20____

National Frozen Yogurt Day

3 Tasks for the day

- ❑ _____
- ❑ _____
- ❑ _____

Today's Doodle

Gratitude Reflection- What is one thing that you are thankful for today?

_____
_____
_____
_____
_____

February **7**, 20____

National Send A Card To Your Friend Day

3 Tasks for the day

- ❑ _____
- ❑ _____
- ❑ _____

Today's Doodle

Gratitude Reflection- What is one thing that you are thankful for today?

_____
_____
_____
_____
_____

Never let anyone or anything dull your shine, your strength is the fuel that keeps it bright.
HKL- Hagman NY

February **8**, *20____*

National Kite Flying Day

3 Tasks for the day

❏ _____
❏ _____
❏ _____

Gratitude Reflection- What is one thing that you are thankful for today?

_____
_____
_____
_____
_____

February **9**, *20____*

Today's Doodle

National Pizza Day

3 Tasks for the day

❏ _____
❏ _____
❏ _____

Gratitude Reflection- What is one thing that you are thankful for today?

_____
_____
_____
_____
_____

A smile is allowing the sun to shine 24/7.
Kathleen Smith- Fort Johnson NY

February **10**, *20___*

National Umbrella Day

3 Tasks for the day

❑ _____
❑ _____
❑ _____

Today's Doodle

Gratitude Reflection- What is one thing that you are thankful for today?

_____
_____
_____
_____
_____

February **11**, *20___*

National Peppermint Patty Day

3 Tasks for the day

❑ _____
❑ _____
❑ _____

Today's Doodle

Gratitude Reflection- What is one thing that you are thankful for today?

_____
_____
_____
_____
_____

Be ready so you don't have to get ready!!! Charles Beekman Jr- Amsteradm NY

February **12**, 20____

Today's Doodle

National Plum Pudding Day

3 Tasks for the day

❑ _____
❑ _____
❑ _____

Gratitude Reflection- What is one thing that you are thankful for today?

_____
_____
_____
_____
_____

February **13**, 20____

Today's Doodle

National Tortellini Day

3 Tasks for the day

❑ _____
❑ _____
❑ _____

Gratitude Reflection- What is one thing that you are thankful for today?

_____
_____
_____
_____
_____

Energy is a Choice. Todd Cetnar Mental Performance Coach- Saratoga Springs NY

February **14,** 20____

Today's Doodle

National Organ Donor Day

3 Tasks for the day

❑ _____
❑ _____
❑ _____

Gratitude Reflection- What is one thing that you are thankful for today?

_____
_____
_____
_____
_____

February **15,** 20____

Today's Doodle

National Gumdrop Day

3 Tasks for the day

❑ _____
❑ _____
❑ _____

Gratitude Reflection- What is one thing that you are thankful for today?

_____
_____
_____
_____
_____

A candle loses nothing when lightning another candle... Smile, it's Contagious.
David Valentin- Brooklyn NY

February **16**, *20____*

Today's Doodle

National Almond Day

3 Tasks for the day

❑ _____
❑ _____
❑ _____

Gratitude Reflection- What is one thing that you are thankful for today?

_____
_____
_____
_____
_____

February **17**, *20____*

Today's Doodle

National Random Act Of Kindness Day

3 Tasks for the day

❑ _____
❑ _____
❑ _____

Gratitude Reflection- What is one thing that you are thankful for today?

_____
_____
_____
_____
_____

*Never cry to give up, cry to keep going and if you fall try and fall on your back, that way
you can see what you have to do to get up.
Tafari Constantine Martin aka Mr. Martin- Amsterdam NY*

February **18**, 20____

Today's Doodle

National Drink Wine Day

3 Tasks for the day

❑ _____
❑ _____
❑ _____

Gratitude Reflection- What is one thing that you are thankful for today?

_____
_____
_____
_____
_____

February **19**, 20____

Today's Doodle

National Chocolate Mint Day

3 Tasks for the day

❑ _____
❑ _____
❑ _____

Gratitude Reflection- What is one thing that you are thankful for today?

_____
_____
_____
_____
_____

Morning Alarm: Be better than what you were yesterday.
Rick Hyde- Charlton NY

February **20**, *20____*

National Love Your Pet Day

Today's Doodle

3 Tasks for the day

❑ _____
❑ _____
❑ _____

Gratitude Reflection- What is one thing that you are thankful for today?

_____
_____
_____
_____
_____

February **21**, *20____*

National Sticky Bun Day

Today's Doodle

3 Tasks for the day

❑ _____
❑ _____
❑ _____

Gratitude Reflection- What is one thing that you are thankful for today?

_____
_____
_____
_____
_____

When we look back at 2020, my hope is that people not only have feelings of regret but are grateful for lessons learned. The importance of family, a simple hug, a lunch with friends, a community always willing to help. Pam Swart- Amsterdam NY

February **22**, *20____*

National Margarita Day

3 Tasks for the day

❑ _____
❑ _____
❑ _____

Today's Doodle

Gratitude Reflection- What is one thing that you are thankful for today?

_____
_____
_____
_____
_____

February **23**, *20____*

National Banana Bread Day

3 Tasks for the day

❑ _____
❑ _____
❑ _____

Today's Doodle

Gratitude Reflection- What is one thing that you are thankful for today?

_____
_____
_____
_____
_____

My greatest wealth is not in the form of money but is the amount of love I have for my family and friends. Sue Poulin- Amsterdam NY

February **24,** 20____

National Tortilla Chip Day

3 Tasks for the day

- ❑ _____
- ❑ _____
- ❑ _____

Gratitude Reflection- What is one thing that you are thankful for today?

_____
_____
_____
_____
_____

February **25,** 20____

National Clam Chowder Day

3 Tasks for the day

- ❑ _____
- ❑ _____
- ❑ _____

Gratitude Reflection- What is one thing that you are thankful for today?

_____
_____
_____
_____
_____

Never wish time away, you can never get it back, embrace every minute of today, tomorrow and always. Life is a gift and it's not forever. Chris Snell- Perth NY

February **26,** 20_____

National Pistachio Day

3 Tasks for the day

- ❏ _____
- ❏ _____
- ❏ _____

Gratitude Reflection- What is one thing that you are thankful for today?

_____
_____
_____
_____
_____

Today's Doodle

February **27,** 20_____

National Retro Day

3 Tasks for the day

- ❏ _____
- ❏ _____
- ❏ _____

Gratitude Reflection- What is one thing that you are thankful for today?

_____
_____
_____
_____
_____

Today's Doodle

*A year can't exist without each individual moment. Don't wait to be happy, to be
fully yourself. Bring your attention like a laser to what makes you feel most alive in the
moment and every day can be a celebration.*
Janis Freeman, Growing Light Wellness And Yoga- Amsterdam NY

February **28**, *20___*   *Today's Doodle*

National Floral Design Day

3 Tasks for the day

❏ _____
❏ _____
❏ _____

Gratitude Reflection- What is one thing that you are thankful for today?

_____
_____
_____
_____
_____

February **29**, *20___*   *Today's Doodle*

National Time Refund Day

3 Tasks for the day

❏ _____
❏ _____
❏ _____

Gratitude Reflection- What is one thing that you are thankful for today?

_____
_____
_____
_____
_____

You can do it, I know you can. Little by little, inch by inch, choice by choice and action by action. HKL- Hagaman NY

March **1**, 20____

National Peanut Butter Lover's Day

3 Tasks for the day

- ❏ _____
- ❏ _____
- ❏ _____

Today's Doodle

Gratitude Reflection- What is one thing that you are thankful for today?

_____
_____
_____
_____
_____

March **2**, 20____

National Old Stuff Day

3 Tasks for the day

- ❏ _____
- ❏ _____
- ❏ _____

Today's Doodle

Gratitude Reflection- What is one thing that you are thankful for today?

_____
_____
_____
_____
_____

Some of my greatest disappointments have turned out to be my greatest blessings. Keep your motives pure and things will work out as they are meant to. Have patience, faith, and let life be. Susie Duross- Johnstown NY

March **3,** *20____*

National Cold Cuts Day

3 Tasks for the day

- ❏ _____
- ❏ _____
- ❏ _____

Today's Doodle

Gratitude Reflection- What is one thing that you are thankful for today?

_____
_____
_____
_____
_____

March **4,** *20____*

National Son's Day

3 Tasks for the day

- ❏ _____
- ❏ _____
- ❏ _____

Today's Doodle

Gratitude Reflection- What is one thing that you are thankful for today?

_____
_____
_____
_____
_____

You are already good enough and you always have been.
Colleen Ripple- Broadalbin NY

March **5**, 20____

National Cheese Doodle Day

3 Tasks for the day

❑ _____
❑ _____
❑ _____

Today's Doodle

Gratitude Reflection- What is one thing that you are thankful for today?

_____
_____
_____
_____

March **6**, 20____

National Oreo Cookie Day

3 Tasks for the day

❑ _____
❑ _____
❑ _____

Today's Doodle

Gratitude Reflection- What is one thing that you are thankful for today?

_____
_____
_____
_____

Attitude is gratitude. I always feel that when I'm grateful- that is all I ever need to
stay positive. Theresa Klausner- Galway NY

*March **7**, 20____*

National Cereal Day

3 Tasks for the day

- ❑ _____
- ❑ _____
- ❑ _____

Today's Doodle

Gratitude Reflection- What is one thing that you are thankful for today?

_____
_____
_____
_____
_____

*March **8**, 20____*

International Women's Day

3 Tasks for the day

- ❑ _____
- ❑ _____
- ❑ _____

Today's Doodle

Gratitude Reflection- What is one thing that you are thankful for today?

_____
_____
_____
_____
_____

Family, friends no matter far or near are the ones we hold most dear. HKL- Hagman NY

March **9**, 20___

Today's Doodle

National Get Over It Day

3 Tasks for the day

- ❑ _____
- ❑ _____
- ❑ _____

Gratitude Reflection- What is one thing that you are thankful for today?

_____
_____
_____
_____

March **10**, 20___

Today's Doodle

National Blueberry Popover Day

3 Tasks for the day

- ❑ _____
- ❑ _____
- ❑ _____

Gratitude Reflection- What is one thing that you are thankful for today?

_____
_____
_____
_____

You are the average of the top 5 people you associate with, choose wisely.
For your future will depend on it. GL- Hagaman NY

March **11**, *20____*

National Johnny Appleseed Day

3 Tasks for the day

❑ _____
❑ _____
❑ _____

Today's Doodle

Gratitude Reflection- What is one thing that you are thankful for today?

_____
_____
_____
_____
_____

March **12**, *20____*

National Plant A Flower Day

3 Tasks for the day

❑ _____
❑ _____
❑ _____

Today's Doodle

Gratitude Reflection- What is one thing that you are thankful for today?

_____
_____
_____
_____
_____

Hope brings you back to the center. Stay grounded in your faith, be true to yourself and never give up. Kristin Petrecky Pasquarelli- Amsterdam NY

38

March **13**, 20____

National Good Samaritan Day

3 Tasks for the day

- ❏ _____
- ❏ _____
- ❏ _____

Gratitude Reflection- What is one thing that you are thankful for today?

_____
_____
_____
_____
_____

March **14**, 20____

Today's Doodle

National Potato Chip Day

3 Tasks for the day

- ❏ _____
- ❏ _____
- ❏ _____

Gratitude Reflection- What is one thing that you are thankful for today?

_____
_____
_____
_____
_____

Step outside your comfort zone and get involved. Brent E. Phetteplace- Hagaman NY

March **15**, *20____*   *Today's Doodle*

National Pears Helene Day

3 Tasks for the day

    ❑ _____
    ❑ _____
    ❑ _____

Gratitude Reflection- What is one thing that you are thankful for today?

_____
_____
_____
_____
_____

March **16**, *20____*   *Today's Doodle*

National Panda Day

3 Tasks for the day

    ❑ _____
    ❑ _____
    ❑ _____

Gratitude Reflection- What is one thing that you are thankful for today?

_____
_____
_____
_____
_____

We can control nothing but ourselves and even that is hard. Sometimes we have to allow people the choice to fail so that they may learn. Susan Casler- Glenn NY

March **17**, 20____

Today's Doodle

National Corned Beef & Cabbage Day

3 Tasks for the day

❑ _____
❑ _____
❑ _____

Gratitude Reflection- What is one thing that you are thankful for today?

_____

_____

_____

_____

_____

March **18**, 20____

Today's Doodle

National Awkward Moments Day

3 Tasks for the day

❑ _____
❑ _____
❑ _____

Gratitude Reflection- What is one thing that you are thankful for today?

_____

_____

_____

_____

_____

It's these moments, when we sometimes feel doubtful, but can remain open to
opportunity, we find the best moments to make us hopeful for our next experiences.
Susan Tower- Fort Johnson

March **19**, 20____

National Let's Laugh Day

3 Tasks for the day

- ❑ _____
- ❑ _____
- ❑ _____

Gratitude Reflection- What is one thing that you are thankful for today?

_____
_____
_____
_____
_____

March **20**, 20____

National Ravioli Day

3 Tasks for the day

- ❑ _____
- ❑ _____
- ❑ _____

Gratitude Reflection- What is one thing that you are thankful for today?

_____
_____
_____
_____
_____

Life doesn't come with a rewind button. Keep moving forward!
Dayton J. King- Mayfield NY

March **21**, 20____   Today's Doodle

National Common Courtesy Day

3 Tasks for the day

- ❏ _____
- ❏ _____
- ❏ _____

Gratitude Reflection- What is one thing that you are thankful for today?

_____
_____
_____
_____
_____

March **22**, 20____   Today's Doodle

National Baravian Crepes Day

3 Tasks for the day

- ❏ _____
- ❏ _____
- ❏ _____

Gratitude Reflection- What is one thing that you are thankful for today?

_____
_____
_____
_____
_____

Take a second and a deep breath. Look around you to see what you have and
want. See what you can do to help others and do it!! Live Life! Action is more
important than talk. Dan Nelli- Amsterdam NY

March **23***, 20____*

National Puppy Day

3 Tasks for the day

- ❑ _____
- ❑ _____
- ❑ _____

Today's Doodle

Gratitude Reflection- What is one thing that you are thankful for today?

_____
_____
_____
_____
_____

March **24***, 20____*

National Cheesesteak Day

3 Tasks for the day

- ❑ _____
- ❑ _____
- ❑ _____

Today's Doodle

Gratitude Reflection- What is one thing that you are thankful for today?

_____
_____
_____
_____
_____

Give from your heart and you will never feel depleted. Robert Camacho- Fort Hunter NY

March **25**, 20____

National Medal Of Honor Day

3 Tasks for the day

❑ _____
❑ _____
❑ _____

Today's Doodle

Gratitude Reflection- What is one thing that you are thankful for today?

_____
_____
_____
_____
_____

March **26**, 20____

National Spinach Day

3 Tasks for the day

❑ _____
❑ _____
❑ _____

Today's Doodle

Gratitude Reflection- What is one thing that you are thankful for today?

_____
_____
_____
_____
_____

Be the reason someone smiles today! ☺ *Anthony Landrio Hagaman- NY*

March **27**, *20____*

National Scribble Day

3 Tasks for the day

- ❑ _____
- ❑ _____
- ❑ _____

Gratitude Reflection- What is one thing that you are thankful for today?

_____
_____
_____
_____
_____

Today's Doodle

March **28**, *20____*

National Black Forest Cake Day

3 Tasks for the day

- ❑ _____
- ❑ _____
- ❑ _____

Gratitude Reflection- What is one thing that you are thankful for today?

_____
_____
_____
_____
_____

Today's Doodle

Don't worry about inspiring people on command...
You'll do it enough accidentally. Jonathan Blake- Johnstown NY

March **29**, 20____

National Mom & Pop Business Owners Day

3 Tasks for the day

- ❑ _____
- ❑ _____
- ❑ _____

Today's Doodle

Gratitude Reflection- What is one thing that you are thankful for today?

_____
_____
_____
_____
_____

March **30**, 20____

National I Am In Control Day

3 Tasks for the day

- ❑ _____
- ❑ _____
- ❑ _____

Today's Doodle

Gratitude Reflection- What is one thing that you are thankful for today?

_____
_____
_____
_____
_____

Expertise, skill, and talent are built on the knowledge gleaned from mistakes along the way. Jessica Rhodes- Tribes Hill NY

March **31**, *20*____

National Tater Day

3 Tasks for the day

❏ _____
❏ _____
❏ _____

Gratitude Reflection- What is one thing that you are thankful for today?

_____
_____
_____
_____
_____

April **1**, *20*____

National April Fools Day

3 Tasks for the day

❏ _____
❏ _____
❏ _____

Gratitude Reflection- What is one thing that you are thankful for today?

_____
_____
_____
_____
_____

Everyday be the BEST you can be! Treat people the way you want to be treated. Always follow your Dreams! Always Dream BIG! Always Reach For The Stars! And NEVER GIVE UP!! You can accomplish anything in the world we live!!
Mike Garrasi- Amsterdam NY

April **2**, 20____

National Peanut Butter & Jelly Day

3 Tasks for the day

- ❏ _____
- ❏ _____
- ❏ _____

Today's Doodle

Gratitude Reflection- What is one thing that you are thankful for today?

_____
_____
_____
_____
_____

April **3**, 20____

World Party Day

3 Tasks for the day

- ❏ _____
- ❏ _____
- ❏ _____

Today's Doodle

Gratitude Reflection- What is one thing that you are thankful for today?

_____
_____
_____
_____
_____

The key to a happy life is finding a way to laugh or make someone else laugh every single day. Kayla Egan-Hines-Broadlabin NY

April **4**, 20____

National Vitamin C Day

3 Tasks for the day

❏ _____
❏ _____
❏ _____

Today's Doodle

Gratitude Reflection- What is one thing that you are thankful for today?

_____
_____
_____
_____
_____

April **5**, 20____

National Caramel Day

3 Tasks for the day

❏ _____
❏ _____
❏ _____

Today's Doodle

Gratitude Reflection- What is one thing that you are thankful for today?

_____
_____
_____
_____
_____

*Always advocate for yourself and those that cannot advocate for themselves.
When it comes to speaking out, I only regret the things I didn't say.
Kelly Quist-Demars- Amsterdam NY*

April **6**, 20____

National Sorry Charlie Day

3 Tasks for the day

❑ _____
❑ _____
❑ _____

Today's Doodle

Gratitude Reflection- What is one thing that you are thankful for today?

_____
_____
_____
_____
_____

April **7**, 20____

National Beer Day

3 Tasks for the day

❑ _____
❑ _____
❑ _____

Today's Doodle

Gratitude Reflection- What is one thing that you are thankful for today?

_____
_____
_____
_____
_____

Family is there for when friends are not. Friends are there for when family is not.
Find your balance. GL- Hagaman NY

April **8**, 20____

Today's Doodle

National Empanada Day

3 Tasks for the day

- ☐ _____
- ☐ _____
- ☐ _____

Gratitude Reflection- What is one thing that you are thankful for today?

_____
_____
_____
_____
_____

April **9**, 20____

Today's Doodle

National Unicorn Day

3 Tasks for the day

- ☐ _____
- ☐ _____
- ☐ _____

Gratitude Reflection- What is one thing that you are thankful for today?

_____
_____
_____
_____
_____

Don't limit yourself to one title, one type, one brand. People are many things in one person, and that is fabulously refreshing. Brie Iannotti- Amsterdam NY

April **10**, 20____

National Siblings Day

3 Tasks for the day

- ❑ _____
- ❑ _____
- ❑ _____

Today's Doodle

Gratitude Reflection- What is one thing that you are thankful for today?

_____
_____
_____
_____
_____

April **11**, 20____

National Pet Day

3 Tasks for the day

- ❑ _____
- ❑ _____
- ❑ _____

Today's Doodle

Gratitude Reflection- What is one thing that you are thankful for today?

_____
_____
_____
_____
_____

Smile Often! Smiles are like sunshine on a cloudy day! Liz Tesiero- Broadalbin NY

April **12,** *20_____*

National Big Wind Day

3 Tasks for the day

- ❏ _____
- ❏ _____
- ❏ _____

Gratitude Reflection- What is one thing that you are thankful for today?

_____
_____
_____
_____
_____

April **13,** *20_____*

National Peach Cobbler Day

3 Tasks for the day

- ❏ _____
- ❏ _____
- ❏ _____

Gratitude Reflection- What is one thing that you are thankful for today?

_____
_____
_____
_____
_____

You can't enter into a new year expecting or hoping for it to be better just because it's new. If you want to view it as a clean slate, cool; but if you want something to change, that's on you. Jen Hazzard- Broadalbin NY

April **14**, 20____

National Pecan Day

3 Tasks for the day

- ❑ _____
- ❑ _____
- ❑ _____

Today's Doodle

Gratitude Reflection- What is one thing that you are thankful for today?

_____
_____
_____
_____
_____

April **15**, 20____

National Tax Day

3 Tasks for the day

- ❑ _____
- ❑ _____
- ❑ _____

Today's Doodle

Gratitude Reflection- What is one thing that you are thankful for today?

_____
_____
_____
_____
_____

A vision not fully developed can be critiqued by someone that can not see the final product. In order for someone to see the picture you must finish the drawing for them to see the big picture. Uncle John- Amsterdam NY

55

April **16,** *20____*

National Orchid Day

3 Tasks for the day

❏ _____
❏ _____
❏ _____

Today's Doodle

Gratitude Reflection- What is one thing that you are thankful for today?

_____
_____
_____
_____
_____

April **17,** *20____*

National Crawfish Day

3 Tasks for the day

❏ _____
❏ _____
❏ _____

Today's Doodle

Gratitude Reflection- What is one thing that you are thankful for today?

_____
_____
_____
_____
_____

We always have choices. We may not like any of them at a specific point in time, especially with the consequences that tag along. However, never allow yourself to think or say, I have no choice. Kara Ulasewicz Travis-Town of Florida NY

April **18**, 20____

National Animal Crackers Day

3 Tasks for the day

- ❏ _____
- ❏ _____
- ❏ _____

Today's Doodle

Gratitude Reflection- What is one thing that you are thankful for today?

_____
_____
_____
_____
_____

April **19**, 20____

National Hanging Out Day

3 Tasks for the day

- ❏ _____
- ❏ _____
- ❏ _____

Today's Doodle

Gratitude Reflection- What is one thing that you are thankful for today?

_____
_____
_____
_____
_____

Don't wait until New Years to make a needed change. Marc LaBahn- Amsterdam NY

April **20**, 20____

National Cheddar Fries Day

3 Tasks for the day

❑ _____
❑ _____
❑ _____

Today's Doodle

Gratitude Reflection- What is one thing that you are thankful for today?

_____
_____
_____
_____
_____

April **21**, 20____

National Kindergarten Day

3 Tasks for the day

❑ _____
❑ _____
❑ _____

Today's Doodle

Gratitude Reflection- What is one thing that you are thankful for today?

_____
_____
_____
_____
_____

Stop focusing on the wishing and wanting but focus on the do-ing and the don't-ing.

Do: Dream	*Don't: Limit yourself*
Do: Write down your goals	*Don't: Be around negative people*
Do: Be brave	*Don't: Be afraid to fail*

HKL-Hagaman NY

April **22**, 20____

Today's Doodle

National Earth Day

3 Tasks for the day

❑ _____
❑ _____
❑ _____

Gratitude Reflection- What is one thing that you are thankful for today?

_____
_____
_____
_____
_____

April **23**, 20____

Today's Doodle

National Cherry Cheesecake Day

3 Tasks for the day

❑ _____
❑ _____
❑ _____

Gratitude Reflection- What is one thing that you are thankful for today?

_____
_____
_____
_____
_____

Be your own advocate, because no one will fight for you harder than you.
Pamela Hart- Gloversville NY

April **24**, *20____*

Today's Doodle

National Pigs In A Blanket Day

3 Tasks for the day

❑ _____
❑ _____
❑ _____

Gratitude Reflection- What is one thing that you are thankful for today?

_____
_____
_____
_____
_____

April **25**, *20____*

Today's Doodle

National Hug A Plumber Day

3 Tasks for the day

❑ _____
❑ _____
❑ _____

Gratitude Reflection- What is one thing that you are thankful for today?

_____
_____
_____
_____
_____

Learn what makes you happy, and visit that place often. Sarah D- Amsterdam NY

April **26**, 20____

National Pretzel Day

Today's Doodle

3 Tasks for the day

- ❏ _____
- ❏ _____
- ❏ _____

Gratitude Reflection- What is one thing that you are thankful for today?

_____
_____
_____
_____
_____

April **27**, 20____

National Tell A Story Day

Today's Doodle

3 Tasks for the day

- ❏ _____
- ❏ _____
- ❏ _____

Gratitude Reflection- What is one thing that you are thankful for today?

_____
_____
_____
_____
_____

Always stick to your word, because your word is your bond and once that bond is broken nothing, not even super glue will make it perfect again.
HKL- Hagaman NY

April **28***, 20*____

Today's Doodle

National Blueberry Pie Day

3 Tasks for the day

- ❑ _____
- ❑ _____
- ❑ _____

Gratitude Reflection- What is one thing that you are thankful for today?

_____
_____
_____
_____
_____

April **29***, 20*____

Today's Doodle

National Peace Rose Day

3 Tasks for the day

- ❑ _____
- ❑ _____
- ❑ _____

Gratitude Reflection- What is one thing that you are thankful for today?

_____
_____
_____
_____
_____

LIFE is A humble Storm. A beautiful yet Dark Patient Monster BORN TO FLOURISH.
K. Vazquez-Amsterdam NY

April **30**, 20____

National Honesty Day

3 Tasks for the day

- ❏ _____
- ❏ _____
- ❏ _____

Today's Doodle

Gratitude Reflection- What is one thing that you are thankful for today?

_____
_____
_____
_____
_____

May **1**, 20____

National Loyalty Day

3 Tasks for the day

- ❏ _____
- ❏ _____
- ❏ _____

Today's Doodle

Gratitude Reflection- What is one thing that you are thankful for today?

_____
_____
_____
_____
_____

All we get is time and choices...choose wisely. Meghan M - Amsterdam NY

May **2**, 20____

National Truffle Day

Today's Doodle

3 Tasks for the day

❑ _____
❑ _____
❑ _____

Gratitude Reflection- What is one thing that you are thankful for today?

_____
_____
_____
_____
_____

May **3**, 20____

National Raspberry Pop Over Day

Today's Doodle

3 Tasks for the day

❑ _____
❑ _____
❑ _____

Gratitude Reflection- What is one thing that you are thankful for today?

_____
_____
_____
_____
_____

Breath in... now breath out... And remember, today, your life has a purpose to still be breathing. Chad Leonard- Broadalbin NY

May **4**, 20____

National StarWars Day

3 Tasks for the day

- ❑ _____
- ❑ _____
- ❑ _____

Gratitude Reflection- What is one thing that you are thankful for today?

_____
_____
_____
_____
_____

May **5**, 20____

Today's Doodle

National Cinco De Mayo Day

3 Tasks for the day

- ❑ _____
- ❑ _____
- ❑ _____

Gratitude Reflection- What is one thing that you are thankful for today?

_____
_____
_____
_____
_____

The gift of time is all a person truly has to give you. Be sure you are compensated, for there is a limit on how much we can give. GL- Hagaman

May **6**, 20____

National Nurses Day

3 Tasks for the day

❏ _____
❏ _____
❏ _____

Today's Doodle

Gratitude Reflection- What is one thing that you are thankful for today?

_____
_____
_____
_____
_____

May **7**, 20____

National Roast Leg Of Lamb Day

3 Tasks for the day

❏ _____
❏ _____
❏ _____

Today's Doodle

Gratitude Reflection- What is one thing that you are thankful for today?

_____
_____
_____
_____
_____

Keep your faith and your sense of humor.
Linda E. Eastman- Broadalbin Christian Bookstore

May **8**, 20____

National Have A Coke Day

Today's Doodle

3 Tasks for the day

❑ _____
❑ _____
❑ _____

Gratitude Reflection- What is one thing that you are thankful for today?

_____
_____
_____
_____
_____

May **9**, 20____

National Sleepover Day

Today's Doodle

3 Tasks for the day

❑ _____
❑ _____
❑ _____

Gratitude Reflection- What is one thing that you are thankful for today?

_____
_____
_____
_____
_____

Every dawn is a new beginning. We may leave behind the resentments of the past without forgetting the injustice. We may believe that within every man lies the capacity for good and have hope. We may expect the perfect calm of Christ's assurance that all will be well. Mark Steven Romani- Albany NY

May **10,** *20____*   *Today's Doodle*

National Clean Up Your Room Day

3 Tasks for the day

    ❑   _____
    ❑   _____
    ❑   _____

Gratitude Reflection- What is one thing that you are thankful for today?

_____
_____
_____
_____
_____

May **11,** *20____*   *Today's Doodle*

National Eat What Your Want Day

3 Tasks for the day

    ❑   _____
    ❑   _____
    ❑   _____

Gratitude Reflection- What is one thing that you are thankful for today?

_____
_____
_____
_____
_____

When things get hot, you've got to stay cool. Victor Giulianelli - Amsterdam NY

May **12**, 20____

National Odometer Day

3 Tasks for the day

☐ _____
☐ _____
☐ _____

Today's Doodle

Gratitude Reflection- What is one thing that you are thankful for today?

_____
_____
_____
_____
_____

May **13**, 20____

National Apple Pie Day

3 Tasks for the day

☐ _____
☐ _____
☐ _____

Today's Doodle

Gratitude Reflection- What is one thing that you are thankful for today?

_____
_____
_____
_____
_____

Own each day by living with purpose and loving with your whole heart.
Amanda Mittler- Town of Florida NY

May **14,** *20____*

National Decency Day

3 Tasks for the day

❑ _____
❑ _____
❑ _____

Today's Doodle

Gratitude Reflection- What is one thing that you are thankful for today?

_____
_____
_____
_____
_____

May **15,** *20____*

National Chocolate Chip Day

3 Tasks for the day

❑ _____
❑ _____
❑ _____

Today's Doodle

Gratitude Reflection- What is one thing that you are thankful for today?

_____
_____
_____
_____
_____

Some people practice you do, others practice I won't do, me; I practice we all can do.
Robert Mendoza- Tribes Hill

May **16,** 20____

National Barbeque Day

3 Tasks for the day

❑ _____
❑ _____
❑ _____

Today's Doodle

Gratitude Reflection- What is one thing that you are thankful for today?

_____
_____
_____
_____
_____

May **17,** 20____

National Cherry Cobbler Day

3 Tasks for the day

❑ _____
❑ _____
❑ _____

Today's Doodle

Gratitude Reflection- What is one thing that you are thankful for today?

_____
_____
_____
_____
_____

You Snooze, You lose. Nancy Carr- Perth NY

May **18**, 20____

Today's Doodle

National Visit Your Relatives Day

3 Tasks for the day

❏ _____
❏ _____
❏ _____

Gratitude Reflection- What is one thing that you are thankful for today?

_____
_____
_____
_____
_____

May **19**, 20____

Today's Doodle

National Devil's Food Cake Day

3 Tasks for the day

❏ _____
❏ _____
❏ _____

Gratitude Reflection- What is one thing that you are thankful for today?

_____
_____
_____
_____
_____

I believe in finding strength in your struggles. When you have faith, hope, and love, sometimes the loss of a loved one can be a little easier knowing their after life is a happy life. Amen. Charisse Perez- Amsterdam NY

May **20**, 20____

Today's Doodle

National Pick Strawberries Day

3 Tasks for the day

- ☐ _____
- ☐ _____
- ☐ _____

Gratitude Reflection- What is one thing that you are thankful for today?

_____
_____
_____
_____

May **21**, 20____

Today's Doodle

National Waitstaff Day

3 Tasks for the day

- ☐ _____
- ☐ _____
- ☐ _____

Gratitude Reflection- What is one thing that you are thankful for today?

_____
_____
_____
_____

In a world of yes and no, be the maybe. Sara- Amsterdam NY

May **22**, 20____

National Vanilla Pudding Day

3 Tasks for the day

❑ _____
❑ _____
❑ _____

Gratitude Reflection- What is one thing that you are thankful for today?

_____
_____
_____
_____
_____

May **23**, 20____

Today's Doodle

National Lucky Penny Day

3 Tasks for the day

❑ _____
❑ _____
❑ _____

Gratitude Reflection- What is one thing that you are thankful for today?

_____
_____
_____
_____
_____

When there's no seeking sympathy, truth's integrity will always hold up.
Tafari Constantine Martin aka Mr. Martin- Amsterdam NY

May **24**, 20____

National Brother's Day

3 Tasks for the day

- ☐ _____
- ☐ _____
- ☐ _____

Today's Doodle

Gratitude Reflection- What is one thing that you are thankful for today?

_____
_____
_____
_____
_____

May **25**, 20____

National Wine Day

3 Tasks for the day

- ☐ _____
- ☐ _____
- ☐ _____

Today's Doodle

Gratitude Reflection- What is one thing that you are thankful for today?

_____
_____
_____
_____
_____

Do not let anyone dull your bright light. If they try to dim your brightness, take a deep breath, you move along and shine on- find your people to appreciate your love, kindness, and light. Mrs. Anne Boles - Gloversville NY

May 26, 20____

National Paper Airplane Day

3 Tasks for the day

- ❏ _____
- ❏ _____
- ❏ _____

Today's Doodle

Gratitude Reflection- What is one thing that you are thankful for today?

_____
_____
_____
_____
_____

May 27, 20____

National Grape Popsicle Day

3 Tasks for the day

- ❏ _____
- ❏ _____
- ❏ _____

Today's Doodle

Gratitude Reflection- What is one thing that you are thankful for today?

_____
_____
_____
_____
_____

We get one body, one life, one mind. Nourish it, love it, respect it, honor it, strengthen it. Treat your body well, it's the only one you have. Michela Mosso- East Rutherford NJ

May **28**, 20___

Today's Doodle

National Brisket Day

3 Tasks for the day

- ❑ _____
- ❑ _____
- ❑ _____

Gratitude Reflection- What is one thing that you are thankful for today?

_____
_____
_____
_____
_____

May **29**, 20___

Today's Doodle

National Paperclip Day

3 Tasks for the day

- ❑ _____
- ❑ _____
- ❑ _____

Gratitude Reflection- What is one thing that you are thankful for today?

_____
_____
_____
_____
_____

There is something that can be learned through every relationship, experience, and interaction. Mike DiMezza-Amsterdam NY

May **30**, 20____

National Creativity Day

3 Tasks for the day

- ❏ _____
- ❏ _____
- ❏ _____

Today's Doodle

Gratitude Reflection- What is one thing that you are thankful for today?

_____
_____
_____
_____
_____

May **31**, 20____

National Smile Day

3 Tasks for the day

- ❏ _____
- ❏ _____
- ❏ _____

Today's Doodle

Gratitude Reflection- What is one thing that you are thankful for today?

_____
_____
_____
_____
_____

You are stronger than you know. Rebecca Hancock- Johnstown NY

June **1**, 20____

National Olive Day

3 Tasks for the day

❑ _____
❑ _____
❑ _____

Today's Doodle

Gratitude Reflection- What is one thing that you are thankful for today?

_____
_____
_____
_____
_____

June **2**, 20____

National Rocky Road Day

3 Tasks for the day

❑ _____
❑ _____
❑ _____

Today's Doodle

Gratitude Reflection- What is one thing that you are thankful for today?

_____
_____
_____
_____
_____

Always be true to yourself, even if it causes discomfort. The greatest changes occur when you exceed limits you never thought possible. Katerina Gaylord-Glenville NY

June **3**, 20____

Today's Doodle

National Repeat Day

3 Tasks for the day

❑ _____
❑ _____
❑ _____

Gratitude Reflection- What is one thing that you are thankful for today?

_____
_____
_____
_____
_____

June **4**, 20____

Today's Doodle

National Hug Your Cat Day

3 Tasks for the day

❑ _____
❑ _____
❑ _____

Gratitude Reflection- What is one thing that you are thankful for today?

_____
_____
_____
_____
_____

The sunshine is like the "glow" on your face! Sandy Scott- Amsterdam NY

June **5**, 20____

National Veggie Burger Day

3 Tasks for the day

❑ _____
❑ _____
❑ _____

Gratitude Reflection- What is one thing that you are thankful for today?

_____
_____
_____
_____
_____

June **6**, 20____

Today's Doodle

National Yo-Yo Day

3 Tasks for the day

❑ _____
❑ _____
❑ _____

Gratitude Reflection- What is one thing that you are thankful for today?

_____
_____
_____
_____
_____

Don't let fear control what you want to do in life and who you want in your life.
Choose love not fear. Priscilla Rogers- Amsterdam NY

June **7**, 20____

National Chocolate Ice Cream Day

3 Tasks for the day

❑ _____
❑ _____
❑ _____

Today's Doodle

Gratitude Reflection- What is one thing that you are thankful for today?

_____
_____
_____
_____
_____

June **8**, 20____

National Best Friends Day

3 Tasks for the day

❑ _____
❑ _____
❑ _____

Today's Doodle

Gratitude Reflection- What is one thing that you are thankful for today?

_____
_____
_____
_____
_____

Your ability to perceive and envision more than what the world offers you is your greatest artistic gift. Your inner creative voice is not audible to others, listen to it and show them the way. Tina Rodriguez- Rotterdam

June **9**, 20____

National Donald Duck Day

3 Tasks for the day

- ❑ _____
- ❑ _____
- ❑ _____

Today's Doodle

Gratitude Reflection- What is one thing that you are thankful for today?

_____
_____
_____
_____
_____

June **10**, 20____

National Egg Roll Day

3 Tasks for the day

- ❑ _____
- ❑ _____
- ❑ _____

Today's Doodle

Gratitude Reflection- What is one thing that you are thankful for today?

_____
_____
_____
_____
_____

Do your due diligence, love unconditionally, replace the hate, be selfless and appreciate all that we do have and take nothing for granted. Godspeed.
Victoria Mosso, RN- Amsterdam NY

June **11**, 20_____

Today's Doodle

National Corn On The Cob Day

3 Tasks for the day

- ❏ _____
- ❏ _____
- ❏ _____

Gratitude Reflection- What is one thing that you are thankful for today?

_____
_____
_____
_____
_____

June **12**, 20_____

Today's Doodle

National Loving Day

3 Tasks for the day

- ❏ _____
- ❏ _____
- ❏ _____

Gratitude Reflection- What is one thing that you are thankful for today?

_____
_____
_____
_____
_____

May the light in your heart be a beacon for others and may our collective glow lead us out of the darkness and into the light. James Forrest FNP-C- Johnstown NY

June **13**, 20____

National Weed Your Garden Day

3 Tasks for the day

- ☐ _____
- ☐ _____
- ☐ _____

Today's Doodle

Gratitude Reflection- What is one thing that you are thankful for today?

_____
_____
_____
_____
_____

June **14**, 20____

National Bourbon Day

3 Tasks for the day

- ☐ _____
- ☐ _____
- ☐ _____

Today's Doodle

Gratitude Reflection- What is one thing that you are thankful for today?

_____
_____
_____
_____
_____

Kindness is more about sowing the seeds and less about the harvest.
Cynthia Forrest, DNP, FNP-C- Johnstown NY

June **15**, 20____

National Smile Power Day

3 Tasks for the day

- ☐ _____
- ☐ _____
- ☐ _____

Today's Doodle

Gratitude Reflection- What is one thing that you are thankful for today?

_____
_____
_____
_____
_____

June **16**, 20____

National Fudge Day

3 Tasks for the day

- ☐ _____
- ☐ _____
- ☐ _____

Today's Doodle

Gratitude Reflection- What is one thing that you are thankful for today?

_____
_____
_____
_____
_____

Smile, it makes the world a better place! Holly Lee- Amsterdam NY

June **17**, 20___

National Stewart's Root Beer Day

3 Tasks for the day

- ❏ _____
- ❏ _____
- ❏ _____

Today's Doodle

Gratitude Reflection- What is one thing that you are thankful for today?

_____
_____
_____
_____
_____

June **18**, 20___

National Go Fishing Day

3 Tasks for the day

- ❏ _____
- ❏ _____
- ❏ _____

Today's Doodle

Gratitude Reflection- What is one thing that you are thankful for today?

_____
_____
_____
_____
_____

To understand what a good year is you have to be shown what a bad year is.
Be thankful always. Karl Baia- Amsterdam NY

June **19**, 20____

Today's Doodle

National Watch Day

3 Tasks for the day

❏ _____
❏ _____
❏ _____

Gratitude Reflection- What is one thing that you are thankful for today?

_____
_____
_____
_____
_____

June **20**, 20____

Today's Doodle

National Vanilla Milkshake Day

3 Tasks for the day

❏ _____
❏ _____
❏ _____

Gratitude Reflection- What is one thing that you are thankful for today?

_____
_____
_____
_____
_____

Smiles are free, Hand them out like life jackets on the Titanic, you might save someone.

Slezak - Amsterdam NY

June **21**, 20____

National Go Skateboarding Day

3 Tasks for the day

- ❏ _____
- ❏ _____
- ❏ _____

Today's Doodle

Gratitude Reflection- What is one thing that you are thankful for today?

_____
_____
_____
_____
_____

June **22**, 20____

National Chocolate Eclair Day

3 Tasks for the day

- ❏ _____
- ❏ _____
- ❏ _____

Today's Doodle

Gratitude Reflection- What is one thing that you are thankful for today?

_____
_____
_____
_____
_____

Be persistently focused on your dream, courageous enough to take the step and success will occur. Christopher Menge- Hagaman NY

June **23**, 20____

National Pink Day

3 Tasks for the day

❏ _____
❏ _____
❏ _____

Gratitude Reflection- What is one thing that you are thankful for today?

_____
_____
_____
_____
_____

Today's Doodle

June **24**, 20____

National Pralines Day

3 Tasks for the day

❏ _____
❏ _____
❏ _____

Gratitude Reflection- What is one thing that you are thankful for today?

_____
_____
_____
_____
_____

Today's Doodle

Everything changes, how we embrace the change is what matters.
Karen Ogborn- Amsterdam NY

June **25**, 20____   *Today's Doodle*

National Strawberry Parfait Day

3 Tasks for the day

- ❏ _____
- ❏ _____
- ❏ _____

Gratitude Reflection- What is one thing that you are thankful for today?

_____
_____
_____
_____
_____

June **26**, 20____   *Today's Doodle*

National Beautician's Day

3 Tasks for the day

- ❏ _____
- ❏ _____
- ❏ _____

Gratitude Reflection- What is one thing that you are thankful for today?

_____
_____
_____
_____
_____

Your sweet smile, a kind word or a simple favor can multiply good vibes far and wide- spread kindness! Sherri Raponi Perth, NY

June **27**, *20____*   *Today's Doodle*

National Sunglasses Day

3 Tasks for the day

- ❏ _____
- ❏ _____
- ❏ _____

Gratitude Reflection- What is one thing that you are thankful for today?

_____
_____
_____
_____
_____

June **28**, *20____*   *Today's Doodle*

National Logistics Day

3 Tasks for the day

- ❏ _____
- ❏ _____
- ❏ _____

Gratitude Reflection- What is one thing that you are thankful for today?

_____
_____
_____
_____
_____

Always strive to be self aware enough to entertain the notion of meaningful change.
J.Ross- Saratoga Springs NY

June **29**, 20____

National Camera Day

Today's Doodle

3 Tasks for the day

❏ _____
❏ _____
❏ _____

Gratitude Reflection- What is one thing that you are thankful for today?

_____
_____
_____
_____
_____

June **30**, 20____

National Meteor Watch Day

Today's Doodle

3 Tasks for the day

❏ _____
❏ _____
❏ _____

Gratitude Reflection- What is one thing that you are thankful for today?

_____
_____
_____
_____
_____

Every situation does not require an immediate solution or response.
Mike DiMezza-Amsterdam NY

July **1**, 20____

National Gingersnap Day

3 Tasks for the day

- ❑ _____
- ❑ _____
- ❑ _____

Today's Doodle

Gratitude Reflection- What is one thing that you are thankful for today?

_____
_____
_____
_____
_____

July **2**, 20____

National Anisette Day

3 Tasks for the day

- ❑ _____
- ❑ _____
- ❑ _____

Today's Doodle

Gratitude Reflection- What is one thing that you are thankful for today?

_____
_____
_____
_____
_____

If it was meant to happen any other way, it would have. You are where you are for a reason.

Erika Iler- Pattersonville- NY

July **3**, 20____

Today's Doodle

National Chocolate Wafer Day

3 Tasks for the day

- ❏ _____
- ❏ _____
- ❏ _____

Gratitude Reflection- What is one thing that you are thankful for today?

_____

_____

_____

_____

_____

July **4**, 20____

Today's Doodle

National Barbecued Spareribs Day

3 Tasks for the day

- ❏ _____
- ❏ _____
- ❏ _____

Gratitude Reflection- What is one thing that you are thankful for today?

_____

_____

_____

_____

_____

Stand Tall and be confident even when you are unsure. Tricia Altieri- Amsterdam NY

July **5**, 20____

National Apple Turnover Day

3 Tasks for the day

- ❏ _____
- ❏ _____
- ❏ _____

Today's Doodle

Gratitude Reflection- What is one thing that you are thankful for today?

_____
_____
_____
_____
_____

July **6**, 20____

National Fried Chicken Day

3 Tasks for the day

- ❏ _____
- ❏ _____
- ❏ _____

Today's Doodle

Gratitude Reflection- What is one thing that you are thankful for today?

_____
_____
_____
_____
_____

Let go of anger and revenge and let kindness and fairness to represent you.
Mo Ghazi- Amsterdam NY

July **7**, 20____

National Dive Bar Day

3 Tasks for the day

- ❑ _____
- ❑ _____
- ❑ _____

Today's Doodle

Gratitude Reflection- What is one thing that you are thankful for today?

_____
_____
_____
_____
_____

July **8**, 20____

National Freezer Pop Day

3 Tasks for the day

- ❑ _____
- ❑ _____
- ❑ _____

Today's Doodle

Gratitude Reflection- What is one thing that you are thankful for today?

_____
_____
_____
_____
_____

So often we think that the manners and actions of one invested individual can't move the needle. But one voice can make a difference and charge people to come together not just for something good but for something even better. Amanda Bearcroft- Fort Hunter NY

July **9**, 20____

National Sugar Cookie Day

3 Tasks for the day

- ❏ _____
- ❏ _____
- ❏ _____

Today's Doodle

Gratitude Reflection- What is one thing that you are thankful for today?

_____
_____
_____
_____
_____

July **10**, 20____

National Kitten Day

3 Tasks for the day

- ❏ _____
- ❏ _____
- ❏ _____

Today's Doodle

Gratitude Reflection- What is one thing that you are thankful for today?

_____
_____
_____
_____
_____

It is time to get more comfortable with vulnerability. It's time to allow yourself some grace. It's time you stop allowing your perceptions and thoughts to define you. It's time to trust the people around you that have proven themselves. Meghan Evans- East Nassau NY

July **11**, *20*____

National Cheer Up The Lonely Day

3 Tasks for the day

- [ ] _____
- [ ] _____
- [ ] _____

Today's Doodle

Gratitude Reflection- What is one thing that you are thankful for today?

_____
_____
_____
_____
_____

July **12**, *20*____

National Pecan Pie Day

3 Tasks for the day

- [ ] _____
- [ ] _____
- [ ] _____

Today's Doodle

Gratitude Reflection- What is one thing that you are thankful for today?

_____
_____
_____
_____
_____

I challenge you today to do something small and kind for someone else. Gifting small joys to someone else's heart will only cultivate a larger joy in your own! HKL Hagaman- NY

July **13**, 20____

National French Fry Day

3 Tasks for the day

- ❑ _____
- ❑ _____
- ❑ _____

Today's Doodle

Gratitude Reflection- What is one thing that you are thankful for today?

_____
_____
_____
_____
_____

July **14**, 20____

National Mac n Cheese Day

3 Tasks for the day

- ❑ _____
- ❑ _____
- ❑ _____

Today's Doodle

Gratitude Reflection- What is one thing that you are thankful for today?

_____
_____
_____
_____
_____

*Treat people the way you would like others to treat your own children... be it a
co worker, employee, or even someone on the street. When you treat people in that way,
it's easy to be kind. Marie Rhodes- Amsterdam NY*

July **15**, *20____*

National Give Something Away Day

3 Tasks for the day

- ❑ _____
- ❑ _____
- ❑ _____

Today's Doodle

Gratitude Reflection- What is one thing that you are thankful for today?

_____

_____

_____

_____

_____

July **16**, *20____*

National Corn Fritters Day

3 Tasks for the day

- ❑ _____
- ❑ _____
- ❑ _____

Today's Doodle

Gratitude Reflection- What is one thing that you are thankful for today?

_____

_____

_____

_____

_____

Things become complicated when you do something for the wrong reason. When you do it for the right reason, everything else falls in place.Frankie Rodriguez- West Charlton NY

July **17**, *20____*

National Lottery Day

3 Tasks for the day

- ❑ _____
- ❑ _____
- ❑ _____

Gratitude Reflection- What is one thing that you are thankful for today?

_____
_____
_____
_____
_____

July **18**, *20____*

Today's Doodle

National Sour Candy Day

3 Tasks for the day

- ❑ _____
- ❑ _____
- ❑ _____

Gratitude Reflection- What is one thing that you are thankful for today?

_____
_____
_____
_____
_____

Time gives us perspective, which illuminates who we are. Be true to you and embrace the care we can give, the opportunities are endless.
Heather Haslun, DNP, FNP-C - Warnerville NY

July **19**, 20____

National Daiquiri Day

3 Tasks for the day

- ❏ _____
- ❏ _____
- ❏ _____

Today's Doodle

Gratitude Reflection- What is one thing that you are thankful for today?

_____
_____
_____
_____
_____

July **20**, 20____

National Moon Day

3 Tasks for the day

- ❏ _____
- ❏ _____
- ❏ _____

Today's Doodle

Gratitude Reflection- What is one thing that you are thankful for today?

_____
_____
_____
_____
_____

Don't should on yourself (Under the category of not letting regret hinder our future and
not beating ourselves up for what we "should" have done)
Abbey Schaufelberg-Ballard- Amsterdam NY

July **21**, 20____

National Be Someone Day

3 Tasks for the day

- ❑ _____
- ❑ _____
- ❑ _____

Today's Doodle

Gratitude Reflection- What is one thing that you are thankful for today?

_____
_____
_____
_____
_____

July **22**, 20____

National Hammock Day

3 Tasks for the day

- ❑ _____
- ❑ _____
- ❑ _____

Today's Doodle

Gratitude Reflection- What is one thing that you are thankful for today?

_____
_____
_____
_____
_____

Do what you say and you'll find that your life will be far less stressful. GL- Hagaman NY

July **23**, 20____

Today's Doodle

National Vanilla Ice Cream Day

3 Tasks for the day

- ❑ _____
- ❑ _____
- ❑ _____

Gratitude Reflection- What is one thing that you are thankful for today?

_____
_____
_____
_____
_____

July **24**, 20____

Today's Doodle

National Cousins Day

3 Tasks for the day

- ❑ _____
- ❑ _____
- ❑ _____

Gratitude Reflection- What is one thing that you are thankful for today?

_____
_____
_____
_____
_____

Your body doesn't slow you down, you slow your body down! Tonya Opalka- Amsterdam NY

July **25,** *20____*

National Merry-Go-Round Day

3 Tasks for the day

❏ _____
❏ _____
❏ _____

Today's Doodle

Gratitude Reflection- What is one thing that you are thankful for today?

_____
_____
_____
_____
_____

July **26,** *20____*

National Bagelfest Day

3 Tasks for the day

❏ _____
❏ _____
❏ _____

Today's Doodle

Gratitude Reflection- What is one thing that you are thankful for today?

_____
_____
_____
_____
_____

Love many, trust few, learn to paddle your own canoe. Lauren Merendo- Amsterdam NY

July **27**, 20____

National Love Is Kind Day

3 Tasks for the day

- ☐ _____
- ☐ _____
- ☐ _____

Today's Doodle

Gratitude Reflection- What is one thing that you are thankful for today?

_____
_____
_____
_____
_____

July **28**, 20____

National Waterpark Day

3 Tasks for the day

- ☐ _____
- ☐ _____
- ☐ _____

Today's Doodle

Gratitude Reflection- What is one thing that you are thankful for today?

_____
_____
_____
_____
_____

When trying to achieve your dreams just remember even the largest ocean started from a single raindrop and one grain of salt. Brooke Ashli V - Amsterdam NY

July **29**, 20____   *Today's Doodle*

National Lasagna Day

3 Tasks for the day

- ❑ _____
- ❑ _____
- ❑ _____

Gratitude Reflection- What is one thing that you are thankful for today?

_____
_____
_____
_____
_____

July **30**, 20____   *Today's Doodle*

National Cheesecake Day

3 Tasks for the day

- ❑ _____
- ❑ _____
- ❑ _____

Gratitude Reflection- What is one thing that you are thankful for today?

_____
_____
_____
_____
_____

*Make manifest your inherent goodness. Use your amazing power for the good of yourself,
others and the entire world. Heal yourself. Heal others. Heal this wounded but still
beautiful world. Live your grace filled gifts and use them for the greater good.
Julie Bablin, PhD, MATS- Altamont NY*

July **31**, *20____*   *Today's Doodle*

National Avocado Day

3 Tasks for the day

    ❑   _____

    ❑   _____

    ❑   _____

Gratitude Reflection- What is one thing that you are thankful for today?

_____

_____

_____

_____

_____

August **1**, *20____*   *Today's Doodle*

National Respect For Parents Day

3 Tasks for the day

    ❑   _____

    ❑   _____

    ❑   _____

Gratitude Reflection- What is one thing that you are thankful for today?

_____

_____

_____

_____

_____

Comfort is safe, nothing exciting is ever created out of safety. It's only when we are uncomfortable that great things happen. Go for it! Frank J. Casler- Glenn NY

August **2**, 20____

National Coloring Book Day

3 Tasks for the day

- ❑ _____
- ❑ _____
- ❑ _____

Gratitude Reflection- What is one thing that you are thankful for today?

_____
_____
_____
_____
_____

Today's Doodle

August **3**, 20____

National Watermelon Day

3 Tasks for the day

- ❑ _____
- ❑ _____
- ❑ _____

Gratitude Reflection- What is one thing that you are thankful for today?

_____
_____
_____
_____
_____

Today's Doodle

We should never social distance. Physical distancing is ok to prevent the spreading of germs, but we're meant to be social creatures and to encourage one another.
Dayton J. King- Mayfield NY

*August **4**, 20____*

National Chocolate Chip Cookie Day

3 Tasks for the day

- ❏ _____
- ❏ _____
- ❏ _____

Today's Doodle

Gratitude Reflection- What is one thing that you are thankful for today?

_____
_____
_____
_____
_____

*August **5**, 20____*

National Oyster Day

3 Tasks for the day

- ❏ _____
- ❏ _____
- ❏ _____

Today's Doodle

Gratitude Reflection- What is one thing that you are thankful for today?

_____
_____
_____
_____
_____

Don't treat others the way you want to be treated. Treat them the way they need or want to be treated. Nancy Carr- Perth NY

August **6**, 20___

National Root Beer Float Day

3 Tasks for the day

❑ _____
❑ _____
❑ _____

Today's Doodle

Gratitude Reflection- What is one thing that you are thankful for today?

_____
_____
_____
_____
_____

August **7**, 20___

National Lighthouse Day

3 Tasks for the day

❑ _____
❑ _____
❑ _____

Today's Doodle

Gratitude Reflection- What is one thing that you are thankful for today?

_____
_____
_____
_____
_____

All our choices have consequences, be sure to own both. HKL- Hagman NY

August **8**, 20____

National Happiness Happens Day

3 Tasks for the day

- ❏ _____
- ❏ _____
- ❏ _____

Today's Doodle

Gratitude Reflection- What is one thing that you are thankful for today?

_____
_____
_____
_____
_____

August **9**, 20____

National Rice Pudding Day

3 Tasks for the day

- ❏ _____
- ❏ _____
- ❏ _____

Today's Doodle

Gratitude Reflection- What is one thing that you are thankful for today?

_____
_____
_____
_____
_____

Don't worry about things as you will never pick the right thing to worry about.
Mary Zellweger- Syracuse NY

August **10**, *20____*

National Lazy Day

3 Tasks for the day

- ❏ _____
- ❏ _____
- ❏ _____

Gratitude Reflection- What is one thing that you are thankful for today?

_____
_____
_____
_____
_____

Today's Doodle

August **11**, *20____*

National Son's and Daughter's Day

3 Tasks for the day

- ❏ _____
- ❏ _____
- ❏ _____

Gratitude Reflection- What is one thing that you are thankful for today?

_____
_____
_____
_____
_____

Today's Doodle

Forget what you thought it was supposed to be, and love what actually is.
Venessa Marotta - Broadalbin NY

August **12**, 20___

National Vinyl Record Day

3 Tasks for the day

- ❑ _____
- ❑ _____
- ❑ _____

Today's Doodle

Gratitude Reflection- What is one thing that you are thankful for today?

_____

_____

_____

_____

_____

August **13**, 20___

National Left Handers Day

3 Tasks for the day

- ❑ _____
- ❑ _____
- ❑ _____

Today's Doodle

Gratitude Reflection- What is one thing that you are thankful for today?

_____

_____

_____

_____

_____

Perseverance in challenging times often means becoming certain through uncertainty familiar with the unfamiliar, and comfortable with the uncomfortable.
Courtney Quackenbush, RN - Fort Plain NY

August **14**, *20____*

National Creamsicle Day

3 Tasks for the day

- ❑ _____
- ❑ _____
- ❑ _____

Gratitude Reflection- What is one thing that you are thankful for today?

_____
_____
_____
_____
_____

Today's Doodle

August **15**, *20____*

National Relaxation Day

3 Tasks for the day

- ❑ _____
- ❑ _____
- ❑ _____

Gratitude Reflection- What is one thing that you are thankful for today?

_____
_____
_____
_____
_____

Today's Doodle

Stop making excuses immediately, it is 100% acceptable to do things you love; it's not SELFish but rather, SELFlove! HKL- Hagman NY

August **16**, 20____

National Tell A Joke Day

3 Tasks for the day

- ❏ _____
- ❏ _____
- ❏ _____

Today's Doodle

Gratitude Reflection- What is one thing that you are thankful for today?

_____
_____
_____
_____
_____

August **17**, 20____

National Nonprofit Day

3 Tasks for the day

- ❏ _____
- ❏ _____
- ❏ _____

Today's Doodle

Gratitude Reflection- What is one thing that you are thankful for today?

_____
_____
_____
_____
_____

You don't always have to do better, sometimes you just need to do different.
Sharlee Berenger- Gloversville NY

August **18**, 20____

National Fajita Day

3 Tasks for the day

- ❏ _____
- ❏ _____
- ❏ _____

Gratitude Reflection- What is one thing that you are thankful for today?

_____
_____
_____
_____
_____

August **19**, 20____

National Soft Serve Ice Cream Day

3 Tasks for the day

- ❏ _____
- ❏ _____
- ❏ _____

Gratitude Reflection- What is one thing that you are thankful for today?

_____
_____
_____
_____
_____

Be kind to all Kinds. Frank Berenger- Gloversville NY

August **20**, *20____*   *Today's Doodle*

National Radio Day

3 Tasks for the day

- ❏ _____
- ❏ _____
- ❏ _____

Gratitude Reflection- What is one thing that you are thankful for today?

_____
_____
_____
_____
_____

August **21**, *20____*   *Today's Doodle*

National Senior Citizens Day

3 Tasks for the day

- ❏ _____
- ❏ _____
- ❏ _____

Gratitude Reflection- What is one thing that you are thankful for today?

_____
_____
_____
_____
_____

I'm not getting old, but my kids are. Bill McCoski- Town of Florida NY

August **22**, *20____*

National Tooth Fairy Day

3 Tasks for the day

- ❏ _____
- ❏ _____
- ❏ _____

Today's Doodle

Gratitude Reflection- What is one thing that you are thankful for today?

_____
_____
_____
_____
_____

August **23**, *20____*

National Cuban Sandwich Day

3 Tasks for the day

- ❏ _____
- ❏ _____
- ❏ _____

Today's Doodle

Gratitude Reflection- What is one thing that you are thankful for today?

_____
_____
_____
_____
_____

Don't spend time with people who think they can fix everything. Spend it with those who give you their shoulder when things aren't fixable. Mahvash Majeed- Albany NY

August **24**, 20____

National Waffle Day

3 Tasks for the day

- ❑ _____
- ❑ _____
- ❑ _____

Today's Doodle

Gratitude Reflection- What is one thing that you are thankful for today?

_____
_____
_____
_____
_____

August **25**, 20____

National Banana Split Day

3 Tasks for the day

- ❑ _____
- ❑ _____
- ❑ _____

Today's Doodle

Gratitude Reflection- What is one thing that you are thankful for today?

_____
_____
_____
_____
_____

There are some stories that need to be told. Stories where lessons are learned and people become "bonded"together. Our bond, pool patch glue. Our lesson.....fluffy people do float! Milly Cozzolino- Gloversville NY

August **26,** *20____*

National Dog Day

3 Tasks for the day

❏ _____
❏ _____
❏ _____

Today's Doodle

Gratitude Reflection- What is one thing that you are thankful for today?

_____
_____
_____
_____
_____

August **27,** *20____*

National Pots De Creme Day

3 Tasks for the day

❏ _____
❏ _____
❏ _____

Today's Doodle

Gratitude Reflection- What is one thing that you are thankful for today?

_____
_____
_____
_____
_____

Kindness makes ones' heart dance. Kathleen Smith- Fort Johnson NY

August **28**, 20____   Today's Doodle

National Red Wine Day

3 Tasks for the day

☐ _____
☐ _____
☐ _____

Gratitude Reflection- What is one thing that you are thankful for today?

_____
_____
_____
_____
_____

August **29**, 20____   Today's Doodle

National Lemon Juice Day

3 Tasks for the day

☐ _____
☐ _____
☐ _____

Gratitude Reflection- What is one thing that you are thankful for today?

_____
_____
_____
_____
_____

If you strive for progress every day, you will find happiness along the way.
Chris Bardequez-Amsterdam NY

August **30**, *20____*   *Today's Doodle*

National Toasted Marshmallow Day

3 Tasks for the day

❑ _____
❑ _____
❑ _____

Gratitude Reflection- What is one thing that you are thankful for today?

_____
_____
_____
_____
_____

August **31**, *20____*   *Today's Doodle*

National Trail Mix Day

3 Tasks for the day

❑ _____
❑ _____
❑ _____

Gratitude Reflection- What is one thing that you are thankful for today?

_____
_____
_____
_____
_____

Don't let fear of failure hold you back from your goals- remember that the journey to creating success is always a series of failures. Jessica Rhodes- Tribes NY

September **1**, 20____

National No Rhyme Nor Reason Day

3 Tasks for the day

- ❑ _____
- ❑ _____
- ❑ _____

Gratitude Reflection- What is one thing that you are thankful for today?

_____
_____
_____
_____
_____

September **2**, 20____

Today's Doodle

National Blueberry Popsicle Day

3 Tasks for the day

- ❑ _____
- ❑ _____
- ❑ _____

Gratitude Reflection- What is one thing that you are thankful for today?

_____
_____
_____
_____
_____

Sometimes we don't need to be fixed, we're not broken pieces all the time. Most times we just need to shift. Shift enough to align, align with who and what best suits you at your current stage of life.   Tafari Constantine Martin aka Mr. Martin- Amsterdam NY

September **3**, 20____

National US Bowling League Day

3 Tasks for the day

❑ _____
❑ _____
❑ _____

Gratitude Reflection- What is one thing that you are thankful for today?

_____
_____
_____
_____
_____

September **4**, 20____

National Wildlife Day

3 Tasks for the day

❑ _____
❑ _____
❑ _____

Gratitude Reflection- What is one thing that you are thankful for today?

_____
_____
_____
_____
_____

Start each day fresh, never carry yesterday's frustrations past midnight. You are the only person who has the power to "set your day off right". HKL Hagman- NY

September **5**, 20____

National Cheese Pizza Day

3 Tasks for the day

- ❑ _____
- ❑ _____
- ❑ _____

Today's Doodle

Gratitude Reflection- What is one thing that you are thankful for today?

_____
_____
_____
_____

September **6**, 20____

National Read A Book Day

3 Tasks for the day

- ❑ _____
- ❑ _____
- ❑ _____

Today's Doodle

Gratitude Reflection- What is one thing that you are thankful for today?

_____
_____
_____
_____

All things in life should be done with humility and kindness.
Lori Schriner, FNP-BC- Fonda NY

*September **7**, 20____*

National Beer Lover's Day

3 Tasks for the day

- ❑ _____
- ❑ _____
- ❑ _____

Today's Doodle

Gratitude Reflection- What is one thing that you are thankful for today?

_____
_____
_____
_____
_____

*September **8**, 20____*

National Ampersand Day

3 Tasks for the day

- ❑ _____
- ❑ _____
- ❑ _____

Today's Doodle

Gratitude Reflection- What is one thing that you are thankful for today?

_____
_____
_____
_____
_____

If you chase your dream you will always be a step behind. If you live your dream, you will be the winner at the finish line. A Delliveneri- Amsterdam NY

September **9**, 20____

National Teddy Bear Day

3 Tasks for the day

❑ _____
❑ _____
❑ _____

Today's Doodle

Gratitude Reflection- What is one thing that you are thankful for today?

_____
_____
_____
_____
_____

September **10**, 20____

National TV Dinner Day

3 Tasks for the day

❑ _____
❑ _____
❑ _____

Today's Doodle

Gratitude Reflection- What is one thing that you are thankful for today?

_____
_____
_____
_____
_____

If you always do the right thing for the right reasons, success and restful nights will always follow. Junell Pasquarelli- Broadalbin NY

September **11**, 20____

National Hot Cross Bun Day

3 Tasks for the day

❑ _____
❑ _____
❑ _____

Today's Doodle

Gratitude Reflection- What is one thing that you are thankful for today?
_____
_____
_____
_____
_____

September **12**, 20____

National Day of Encouragement Day

3 Tasks for the day

❑ _____
❑ _____
❑ _____

Today's Doodle

Gratitude Reflection- What is one thing that you are thankful for today?
_____
_____
_____
_____
_____

Do the hard right thing, not the easy wrong thing. Juan Soler Jr.-Broadalbin NY

September **13**, 20____

National Peanut Day

3 Tasks for the day

- ☐ _____
- ☐ _____
- ☐ _____

Today's Doodle

Gratitude Reflection- What is one thing that you are thankful for today?

_____
_____
_____
_____
_____

September **14**, 20____

National Live Creative Day

3 Tasks for the day

- ☐ _____
- ☐ _____
- ☐ _____

Today's Doodle

Gratitude Reflection- What is one thing that you are thankful for today?

_____
_____
_____
_____
_____

I choose...To live by choice. To make changes. To forgive. To remember. To be thankful. To be brave. To be present. Fear is a reaction but courage is a decision.
Julie Anne- Whipple Warrior '13 -12010

September **15**, 20____

National Linguine Day

3 Tasks for the day

- ❏ _____
- ❏ _____
- ❏ _____

Today's Doodle

Gratitude Reflection- What is one thing that you are thankful for today?

_____
_____
_____
_____
_____

September **16**, 20____

National Guacamole Day

3 Tasks for the day

- ❏ _____
- ❏ _____
- ❏ _____

Today's Doodle

Gratitude Reflection- What is one thing that you are thankful for today?

_____
_____
_____
_____
_____

Our attitudes can spark chain reactions, aim to be the first domino. Spread positivity, make others smile, show compassion, and do what you can to make a positive difference in your life and in the lives of others. Watch how quickly others follow. Nicole Heck- Broadalbin NY

September **17**, 20____

Today's Doodle

National Apple Dumpling Day

3 Tasks for the day

- ❑ _____
- ❑ _____
- ❑ _____

Gratitude Reflection- What is one thing that you are thankful for today?

_____
_____
_____
_____
_____

September **18**, 20____

Today's Doodle

National Cheeseburger Day

3 Tasks for the day

- ❑ _____
- ❑ _____
- ❑ _____

Gratitude Reflection- What is one thing that you are thankful for today?

_____
_____
_____
_____
_____

To find the meaning of life, live in a way that makes even the most ordinary moments feel meaningful. Dani Whelly- Amsterdam NY

September **19**, 20____

National Talk Like A Pirate Day

3 Tasks for the day

❑ _____
❑ _____
❑ _____

Today's Doodle

Gratitude Reflection- What is one thing that you are thankful for today?

_____
_____
_____
_____
_____

September **20**, 20____

National String Cheese Day

3 Tasks for the day

❑ _____
❑ _____
❑ _____

Today's Doodle

Gratitude Reflection- What is one thing that you are thankful for today?

_____
_____
_____
_____
_____

Have you ever noticed how some mornings are green light days and others are red light days?
Don't get frustrated on the red light days or try to "run the light". Instead, just breath, and
let it be a reminder that pauses in the busyness of our lives are healthy and important!
Susie Duross- Johnstown NY

September **21**, 20____

National Chai Day

3 Tasks for the day

- ❑ _____
- ❑ _____
- ❑ _____

Today's Doodle

Gratitude Reflection- What is one thing that you are thankful for today?

_____
_____
_____
_____
_____

September **22**, 20____

National Ice Cream Cone Day

3 Tasks for the day

- ❑ _____
- ❑ _____
- ❑ _____

Today's Doodle

Gratitude Reflection- What is one thing that you are thankful for today?

_____
_____
_____
_____
_____

We are making memories, cause when it's all over and we made it through it, it makes for a good story. Bob Snell- Perth NY

September **23**, 20____

National Teal Talk Day

3 Tasks for the day

- ❑ _____
- ❑ _____
- ❑ _____

Today's Doodle

Gratitude Reflection- What is one thing that you are thankful for today?

_____
_____
_____
_____
_____

September **24**, 20____

National Punctuation Day

3 Tasks for the day

- ❑ _____
- ❑ _____
- ❑ _____

Today's Doodle

Gratitude Reflection- What is one thing that you are thankful for today?

_____
_____
_____
_____
_____

Forward is the best direction. Eric "Ike" Pantalone- Amsterdam NY

September **25**, 20____

National One-Hit Wonder Day

3 Tasks for the day

- ❑ _____
- ❑ _____
- ❑ _____

Today's Doodle

Gratitude Reflection- What is one thing that you are thankful for today?

_____
_____
_____
_____
_____

September **26**, 20____

National Pancake Day

3 Tasks for the day

- ❑ _____
- ❑ _____
- ❑ _____

Today's Doodle

Gratitude Reflection- What is one thing that you are thankful for today?

_____
_____
_____
_____
_____

It takes focus and optimism to look beyond the shortfalls of the present to shape what is yet to come.   Ann Thane- Amsterdam NY

September **27**, 20____

National Chocolate Milk Day

3 Tasks for the day

- ❏ _____
- ❏ _____
- ❏ _____

Gratitude Reflection- What is one thing that you are thankful for today?

_____
_____
_____
_____
_____

September **28**, 20____

National Good Neighbor Day

3 Tasks for the day

- ❏ _____
- ❏ _____
- ❏ _____

Gratitude Reflection- What is one thing that you are thankful for today?

_____
_____
_____
_____
_____

Failing is not failing unless you quit; that is NOT an option! Failing is a journey to prepare for something more awesome. Keep Trying! HKL-Hagman NY

September **29**, 20____   Today's Doodle

National Coffee Day

3 Tasks for the day

- ☐ _____
- ☐ _____
- ☐ _____

Gratitude Reflection- What is one thing that you are thankful for today?

_____
_____
_____
_____
_____

September **30**, 20____   Today's Doodle

National Love People Day

3 Tasks for the day

- ☐ _____
- ☐ _____
- ☐ _____

Gratitude Reflection- What is one thing that you are thankful for today?

_____
_____
_____
_____
_____

The simple things in life- taking a walk, making a meal, cuddling on the couch- are underrated. Jessica Rhodes- Tribes Hill

October **1**, 20____

National Hair Day

3 Tasks for the day

- ☐ _____
- ☐ _____
- ☐ _____

Today's Doodle

Gratitude Reflection- What is one thing that you are thankful for today?

_____
_____
_____
_____
_____

October **2**, 20____

National Fried Scallops Day

3 Tasks for the day

- ☐ _____
- ☐ _____
- ☐ _____

Today's Doodle

Gratitude Reflection- What is one thing that you are thankful for today?

_____
_____
_____
_____
_____

One Breath at a time, one step at a time. Alison Pepe- Amsterdam NY

October 3, 20___

National Techies Day

3 Tasks for the day

- ❑ _____
- ❑ _____
- ❑ _____

Today's Doodle

Gratitude Reflection- What is one thing that you are thankful for today?

_____
_____
_____
_____
_____

October 4, 20___

National Taco Day

3 Tasks for the day

- ❑ _____
- ❑ _____
- ❑ _____

Today's Doodle

Gratitude Reflection- What is one thing that you are thankful for today?

_____
_____
_____
_____
_____

YOU have the greatest control of how successful YOU are. Dayton J. King Mayfield- NY

October **5**, 20____

National Get Funky Day

3 Tasks for the day

- ❑ _____
- ❑ _____
- ❑ _____

Gratitude Reflection- What is one thing that you are thankful for today?

_____
_____
_____
_____
_____

October **6**, 20____

Today's Doodle

National Noodle Day

3 Tasks for the day

- ❑ _____
- ❑ _____
- ❑ _____

Gratitude Reflection- What is one thing that you are thankful for today?

_____
_____
_____
_____
_____

There is always a solution, it may not be something you love, but it is always there.
Mike DiMezza- Amsterdam NY

October **7**, 20____

National Inner Beauty Day

3 Tasks for the day

- ❑ _____
- ❑ _____
- ❑ _____

Today's Doodle

Gratitude Reflection- What is one thing that you are thankful for today?

_____
_____
_____
_____
_____

October **8**, 20____

National Pierogi Day

3 Tasks for the day

- ❑ _____
- ❑ _____
- ❑ _____

Today's Doodle

Gratitude Reflection- What is one thing that you are thankful for today?

_____
_____
_____
_____
_____

Life will always throw curveballs at you. Things change and people change. The most important thing you can do for yourself is always stay true to who you are and never sacrifice that for anyone. Chrissy P.-Amsterdam NY

October **9**, 20____

National Moldy Cheese Day

3 Tasks for the day

- ❑ _____
- ❑ _____
- ❑ _____

Today's Doodle

Gratitude Reflection- What is one thing that you are thankful for today?

_____
_____
_____
_____
_____

October **10**, 20____

National Angel Foodcake Day

3 Tasks for the day

- ❑ _____
- ❑ _____
- ❑ _____

Today's Doodle

Gratitude Reflection- What is one thing that you are thankful for today?

_____
_____
_____
_____
_____

Look on the bright side, it's easier to see things over there.
Jennifer Mehling, FNP- Ballston Spa NY

October **11**, 20___

National Sausage Pizza Day

3 Tasks for the day

- ❏ _____
- ❏ _____
- ❏ _____

Today's Doodle

Gratitude Reflection- What is one thing that you are thankful for today?

_____
_____
_____
_____
_____

October **12**, 20___

National Savings Day

3 Tasks for the day

- ❏ _____
- ❏ _____
- ❏ _____

Today's Doodle

Gratitude Reflection- What is one thing that you are thankful for today?

_____
_____
_____
_____
_____

You have to believe in something. Why not believe in yourself and watch what happens?
You already know what it feels like to see someone you believe in achieve their goals,
imagine that double excitement! Believe in YOU! HKL- Hagaman NY

October **13**, *20____*

National Train Your Brain Day

3 Tasks for the day

❏ _____
❏ _____
❏ _____

Today's Doodle

Gratitude Reflection- What is one thing that you are thankful for today?

_____
_____
_____
_____
_____

October **14**, *20____*

National Dessert Day

3 Tasks for the day

❏ _____
❏ _____
❏ _____

Today's Doodle

Gratitude Reflection- What is one thing that you are thankful for today?

_____
_____
_____
_____
_____

It's time to choose whether or not you'll allow your past experiences to dictate your current mindset. It's time to be present. It's time to live.
Meghan Evans- East Nassau- NY

October **15,** *20___*

National Cheese Curd Day

3 Tasks for the day

❑ _____
❑ _____
❑ _____

Today's Doodle

Gratitude Reflection- What is one thing that you are thankful for today?

_____
_____
_____
_____
_____

October **16,** *20___*

National Sports Day

3 Tasks for the day

❑ _____
❑ _____
❑ _____

Today's Doodle

Gratitude Reflection- What is one thing that you are thankful for today?

_____
_____
_____
_____
_____

Bad experiences don't have to be just bad experiences. The purpose of life is not to be happy, it's to grow as a person. Erin E. Salie, LFD- Schenectady NY

October **17**, *20____*

National Pasta Day

3 Tasks for the day

❑ _____
❑ _____
❑ _____

Today's Doodle

Gratitude Reflection- What is one thing that you are thankful for today?

_____
_____
_____
_____
_____

October **18**, *20____*

National Exascale Day

3 Tasks for the day

❑ _____
❑ _____
❑ _____

Today's Doodle

Gratitude Reflection- What is one thing that you are thankful for today?

_____
_____
_____
_____
_____

Just because you can, does not mean you should. With every decision you face, count the cost to your life, your loved ones, your sense of balance. Be thoughtful about steps you take and protect what matters. Sarah Wilson-Sparrow, Delanson, NY

October **19**, 20____

National Seafood Bisque Day

3 Tasks for the day

- ❑ _____
- ❑ _____
- ❑ _____

Today's Doodle

Gratitude Reflection- What is one thing that you are thankful for today?

_____
_____
_____
_____
_____

October **20**, 20____

National Youth Confidence Day

3 Tasks for the day

- ❑ _____
- ❑ _____
- ❑ _____

Today's Doodle

Gratitude Reflection- What is one thing that you are thankful for today?

_____
_____
_____
_____
_____

Inspire others with your desire... you gotta light the match to start the fire.
A Delliveneri- Amsterdam NY

October **21**, 20____   *Today's Doodle*

National Pumpkin Cheesecake Day

3 Tasks for the day

    ❏ _____
    ❏ _____
    ❏ _____

Gratitude Reflection- What is one thing that you are thankful for today?

_____
_____
_____
_____
_____

October **22**, 20____   *Today's Doodle*

National Nut Day

3 Tasks for the day

    ❏ _____
    ❏ _____
    ❏ _____

Gratitude Reflection- What is one thing that you are thankful for today?

_____
_____
_____
_____
_____

Always be true to yourself , because you're the best version of you.
Sharlee Berenger- Gloversville NY

October **23**, 20____   *Today's Doodle*

National Boston Cream Pie Day

3 Tasks for the day

❑ _____
❑ _____
❑ _____

Gratitude Reflection- What is one thing that you are thankful for today?

_____
_____
_____
_____
_____

October **24**, 20____   *Today's Doodle*

National Food Day

3 Tasks for the day

❑ _____
❑ _____
❑ _____

Gratitude Reflection- What is one thing that you are thankful for today?

_____
_____
_____
_____
_____

You Best You Can. Lori Mucilli- Amsterdam NY

October **25,** *20____*

National Greasy Food Day

3 Tasks for the day

- ❑ _____
- ❑ _____
- ❑ _____

Today's Doodle

Gratitude Reflection- What is one thing that you are thankful for today?

_____
_____
_____
_____
_____

October **26,** *20____*

National Day Of The Deployed Day

3 Tasks for the day

- ❑ _____
- ❑ _____
- ❑ _____

Today's Doodle

Gratitude Reflection- What is one thing that you are thankful for today?

_____
_____
_____
_____
_____

Your life book starts blank. Love the character, don't skip chapters, and take
chances. Always start each page with love and compassion!
Kelly Flewelling- Providence NY

October **27**, 20____

National Black Cat Day

3 Tasks for the day

- ❑ _____
- ❑ _____
- ❑ _____

Today's Doodle

Gratitude Reflection- What is one thing that you are thankful for today?

_____
_____
_____
_____
_____

October **28**, 20____

National Chocolate Day

3 Tasks for the day

- ❑ _____
- ❑ _____
- ❑ _____

Today's Doodle

Gratitude Reflection- What is one thing that you are thankful for today?

_____
_____
_____
_____
_____

God is good.
Great Grandmother Lillian Bushnow- Heaven's Gates

October **29**, 20____

National Cat Day

3 Tasks for the day

☐ _____
☐ _____
☐ _____

Today's Doodle

Gratitude Reflection- What is one thing that you are thankful for today?

_____
_____
_____
_____
_____

October **30**, 20____

National Candy Corn Day

3 Tasks for the day

☐ _____
☐ _____
☐ _____

Today's Doodle

Gratitude Reflection- What is one thing that you are thankful for today?

_____
_____
_____
_____
_____

Find your passion in life and pursue it, life is short. Mark Perfetti- Amsterdam NY

October **31**, 20____   *Today's Doodle*

National Caramel Apple Day

3 Tasks for the day

- ❏ _____
- ❏ _____
- ❏ _____

Gratitude Reflection- What is one thing that you are thankful for today?

_____
_____
_____
_____
_____

November **1**, 20____   *Today's Doodle*

National Author's Day

3 Tasks for the day

- ❏ _____
- ❏ _____
- ❏ _____

Gratitude Reflection- What is one thing that you are thankful for today?

_____
_____
_____
_____
_____

2020 has taught us something, it's the value of leaning into our closest circle.
Jessica Rhodes- Tribes Hill

November **2**, *20____*

National Deviled Egg Day

3 Tasks for the day

- ❏ _____
- ❏ _____
- ❏ _____

Today's Doodle

Gratitude Reflection- What is one thing that you are thankful for today?

_____
_____
_____
_____
_____

November **3**, *20____*

National Sandwich Day

3 Tasks for the day

- ❏ <u>Cheers on my Birthday</u> 😊
- ❏ _____
- ❏ _____

Today's Doodle

Gratitude Reflection- What is one thing that you are thankful for today?

_____
_____
_____
_____
_____

LIFE
L Live, Laugh, Love
I   Inquisitive, never lose your sense of wonder
F Forgive, there is enough hatred in the world
E Enjoy the little things in life
LIFE is a journey, you are in the driver sea, Enjoy the ride!
Deb Crisalli- Amsterdam NY

November **4**, 20____

National Candy Day

3 Tasks for the day

- ☐ _____
- ☐ _____
- ☐ _____

Today's Doodle

Gratitude Reflection- What is one thing that you are thankful for today?

_____
_____
_____
_____
_____

November **5**, 20____

National Doughnut Day

3 Tasks for the day

- ☐ _____
- ☐ _____
- ☐ _____

Today's Doodle

Gratitude Reflection- What is one thing that you are thankful for today?

_____
_____
_____
_____
_____

You can quote the good book or you can quote a scripture but how you treat people in life actually paints God's picture. A Delliveneri- Amsterdam NY

November **6**, 20____

National Nachos Day

Today's Doodle

3 Tasks for the day

❏ _____
❏ _____
❏ _____

Gratitude Reflection- What is one thing that you are thankful for today?

_____
_____
_____
_____
_____

November **7**, 20____

National Bittersweet Chocolate W/ Almonds Day

Today's Doodle

3 Tasks for the day

❏ _____
❏ _____
❏ _____

Gratitude Reflection- What is one thing that you are thankful for today?

_____
_____
_____
_____
_____

Smiles can say a lot. Go out today and have positive conversations.
Margaret Woodward- Central Square

November **8**, *20____*

National Cappuccino Day

3 Tasks for the day

Today's Doodle

- ☐ _____
- ☐ _____
- ☐ _____

Gratitude Reflection- What is one thing that you are thankful for today?

_____
_____
_____
_____
_____

November **9**, *20____*

National Scrapple Day

3 Tasks for the day

Today's Doodle

- ☐ _____
- ☐ _____
- ☐ _____

Gratitude Reflection- What is one thing that you are thankful for today?

_____
_____
_____
_____
_____

GROW WHERE YOU ARE PLANTED- Brya A. Berning- Schenectady NY

November **10**, *20____*   *Today's Doodle*

National Forget-Me-Not Day

3 Tasks for the day

    ❏ _____
    ❏ _____
    ❏ _____

Gratitude Reflection- What is one thing that you are thankful for today?

_____
_____
_____
_____
_____

November **11**, *20____*   *Today's Doodle*

National Veterans Day

3 Tasks for the day

    ❏ _____
    ❏ _____
    ❏ _____

Gratitude Reflection- What is one thing that you are thankful for today?

_____
_____
_____
_____
_____

Always pay it forward and never look back. Nicole Baez- Fonda NY

November **12**, 20____

National Chicken Soup For The Soul Day

3 Tasks for the day

❑ _____
❑ _____
❑ _____

Today's Doodle

Gratitude Reflection- What is one thing that you are thankful for today?

_____
_____
_____
_____
_____

November **13**, 20____

National World Kindness Day

3 Tasks for the day

❑ _____
❑ _____
❑ _____

Today's Doodle

Gratitude Reflection- What is one thing that you are thankful for today?

_____
_____
_____
_____
_____

Each day is a new opportunity toward yet another astounding step toward Self-realization.
Eileen Irene Mazanek Santiago- Amsterdam NY

November **14**, *20____*   *Today's Doodle*

National Pickle Day

3 Tasks for the day

- ❑ _____
- ❑ _____
- ❑ _____

Gratitude Reflection- What is one thing that you are thankful for today?

_____
_____
_____
_____
_____

November **15**, *20____*   *Today's Doodle*

National Clean Out Your Refrigerator Day

3 Tasks for the day

- ❑ _____
- ❑ _____
- ❑ _____

Gratitude Reflection- What is one thing that you are thankful for today?

_____
_____
_____
_____
_____

Sometimes you just have to dig into your soul when you are sad. You will feel something pull the hell at that heart in there...that's when you know you're human and you're not so much alone, when the tears come out. It's an Angel hugging you. So cry when you need to. Shannon Reksc- Hagman NY

November **16**, 20____

National Button Day

3 Tasks for the day

- ☐ _____
- ☐ _____
- ☐ _____

Today's Doodle

Gratitude Reflection- What is one thing that you are thankful for today?

_____
_____
_____
_____
_____

November **17**, 20____

National Homemade Bread Day

3 Tasks for the day

- ☐ _____
- ☐ _____
- ☐ _____

Today's Doodle

Gratitude Reflection- What is one thing that you are thankful for today?

_____
_____
_____
_____
_____

Shuffle your feet. Lose your seat. Nancy Carr- Perth NY

November **18**, 20____

National Vichyssoise Day

3 Tasks for the day

- ❑ _____
- ❑ _____
- ❑ _____

Today's Doodle

Gratitude Reflection- What is one thing that you are thankful for today?

_____
_____
_____
_____
_____

November **19**, 20____

National Play Monopoly Day

3 Tasks for the day

- ❑ _____
- ❑ _____
- ❑ _____

Today's Doodle

Gratitude Reflection- What is one thing that you are thankful for today?

_____
_____
_____
_____
_____

Stop searching for inspiration, be yourself and you'll soon find out it's been there all along. Joe Leone-Amsterdam NY

November **20**, 20____

Today's Doodle

National Peanut Butter Fudge Day

3 Tasks for the day

- ❑ _____
- ❑ _____
- ❑ _____

Gratitude Reflection- What is one thing that you are thankful for today?

_____
_____
_____
_____
_____

November **21**, 20____

Today's Doodle

National Stuffing Day

3 Tasks for the day

- ❑ _____
- ❑ _____
- ❑ _____

Gratitude Reflection- What is one thing that you are thankful for today?

_____
_____
_____
_____
_____

Never, ever underestimate the power of a deep, cleansing breath.
Marianne Reid Schrom- Glenville NY

November **22**, 20____

National Cranberry Relish Day

3 Tasks for the day

- ❑ _____
- ❑ _____
- ❑ _____

Today's Doodle

Gratitude Reflection- What is one thing that you are thankful for today?

_____
_____
_____
_____
_____

November **23** 20____

National Espresso Day

3 Tasks for the day

- ❑ _____
- ❑ _____
- ❑ _____

Today's Doodle

Gratitude Reflection- What is one thing that you are thankful for today?

_____
_____
_____
_____
_____

Wield your awesome power for the betterment of the entire world. Be your true and authentic self. Live your life with gratitude. Be amazing! Julie Bablin, PhD, MATS- Altamont NY

November **24**, 20____

National Sardines Day

3 Tasks for the day

- ❑ _____
- ❑ _____
- ❑ _____

Today's Doodle

Gratitude Reflection- What is one thing that you are thankful for today?

_____
_____
_____
_____
_____

November **25**, 20____

National Shopping Reminder Day

3 Tasks for the day

- ❑ _____
- ❑ _____
- ❑ _____

Today's Doodle

Gratitude Reflection- What is one thing that you are thankful for today?

_____
_____
_____
_____
_____

Footprints...Are your unique imprint on life. Make sure yours are those others strive to walk in. Michele Tomlinson-Amsterdam NY

November **26**, 20____   *Today's Doodle*

National Cake Day

3 Tasks for the day

- ❏ _____
- ❏ _____
- ❏ _____

Gratitude Reflection- What is one thing that you are thankful for today?

_____
_____
_____
_____
_____

November **27**, 20____   *Today's Doodle*

National Craft Jerky Day

3 Tasks for the day

- ❏ _____
- ❏ _____
- ❏ _____

Gratitude Reflection- What is one thing that you are thankful for today?

_____
_____
_____
_____
_____

If you choose to make smart choices and stay safe now your year will be much better by the end and you will have many more years to make memorable moments.
Michele Perry- Scotia NY

November **28**, 20___

National French Toast Day

3 Tasks for the day

- ❑ _____
- ❑ _____
- ❑ _____

Today's Doodle

Gratitude Reflection- What is one thing that you are thankful for today?

_____
_____
_____
_____

November **29**, 20___

National Electronic Greetings Day

3 Tasks for the day

- ❑ _____
- ❑ _____
- ❑ _____

Today's Doodle

Gratitude Reflection- What is one thing that you are thankful for today?

_____
_____
_____
_____

I am brave, smart, and kind. I believe In myself. I can do it. I am confident.
Anne And Lorenzo Boles- Gloversville NY

November **30**, *20____*

National Personal Space Day

3 Tasks for the day

- ❑ _____
- ❑ _____
- ❑ _____

Today's Doodle

Gratitude Reflection- What is one thing that you are thankful for today?

_____
_____
_____
_____
_____

December **1**, *20____*

National Pie Day

3 Tasks for the day

- ❑ _____
- ❑ _____
- ❑ _____

Today's Doodle

Gratitude Reflection- What is one thing that you are thankful for today?

_____
_____
_____
_____
_____

Your only limit is your own mind. Elizabeth Close- Amsterdam NY

December **2**, *20____*

National Mutt Day

3 Tasks for the day

- ❑ _____
- ❑ _____
- ❑ _____

Today's Doodle

Gratitude Reflection- What is one thing that you are thankful for today?

_____

_____

_____

_____

_____

December **3**, *20____*

National Roof Over Your Head Day

3 Tasks for the day

- ❑ _____
- ❑ _____
- ❑ _____

Today's Doodle

Gratitude Reflection- What is one thing that you are thankful for today?

_____

_____

_____

_____

_____

Do not allow negativity or toxic people to consume your minutes. After all, it is suggested to cut off split ends often! HKL- Hagaman NY

*December **4**, 20____*

National Cookie Day

Today's Doodle

3 Tasks for the day

- ❏ _____
- ❏ _____
- ❏ _____

Gratitude Reflection- What is one thing that you are thankful for today?

_____
_____
_____
_____
_____

*December **5**, 20____*

National Bathtub Party Day

Today's Doodle

3 Tasks for the day

- ❏ _____
- ❏ _____
- ❏ _____

Gratitude Reflection- What is one thing that you are thankful for today?

_____
_____
_____
_____
_____

It's time to appreciate the miracle that is your life. It's Time to give yourself credit for the powerhouse you are. It's time to treat your body like a temple.

Meghan Evans- East Nassau NY

December **6**, 20____

National Microwave Oven Day

3 Tasks for the day

❑ _____
❑ _____
❑ _____

Today's Doodle

Gratitude Reflection- What is one thing that you are thankful for today?

_____
_____
_____
_____
_____

December **7**, 20____

National Cotton Candy Day

3 Tasks for the day

❑ _____
❑ _____
❑ _____

Today's Doodle

Gratitude Reflection- What is one thing that you are thankful for today?

_____
_____
_____
_____
_____

No matter the situation, think positive, be positive, speak the positive.
Tara-Fulton County NY

December **8**, 20____

National Brownie Day

3 Tasks for the day

❑ _____
❑ _____
❑ _____

Gratitude Reflection- What is one thing that you are thankful for today?

_____
_____
_____
_____
_____

December **9**, 20____

National Pastry Day

3 Tasks for the day

❑ _____
❑ _____
❑ _____

Today's Doodle

Gratitude Reflection- What is one thing that you are thankful for today?

_____
_____
_____
_____
_____

While the last past year was certainly challenging, it was also a year of growth, hope, strength and gratitude. It's during the times of crisis and turbulence that our weaknesses become strengths and our fears become courage. Donna DeNeuville- Broadalbin NY

December **10**, 20___

National Human Rights Day

3 Tasks for the day

- ❑ _____
- ❑ _____
- ❑ _____

Today's Doodle

Gratitude Reflection- What is one thing that you are thankful for today?

_____
_____
_____
_____
_____

December **11**, 20___

National App Day

3 Tasks for the day

- ❑ _____
- ❑ _____
- ❑ _____

Today's Doodle

Gratitude Reflection- What is one thing that you are thankful for today?

_____
_____
_____
_____
_____

I'm covered in Gods' grace! Beth Allen- Mayfield NY

December **12**, *20____*

National Poinsettia Day

3 Tasks for the day

❑ _____
❑ _____
❑ _____

Today's Doodle

Gratitude Reflection- What is one thing that you are thankful for today?

_____
_____
_____
_____
_____

December **13**, *20____*

National Cocoa Day

3 Tasks for the day

❑ _____
❑ _____
❑ _____

Today's Doodle

Gratitude Reflection- What is one thing that you are thankful for today?

_____
_____
_____
_____
_____

God's Will being done is giving us strength and faith to carry on during our most difficult times. Lori Tessiero-Semkiw- Town of Glen

December **14**, 20____

National Monkey Day

Today's Doodle

3 Tasks for the day

☐ _____
☐ _____
☐ _____

Gratitude Reflection- What is one thing that you are thankful for today?

_____
_____
_____
_____
_____

December **15**, 20____

National Cupcake Day

Today's Doodle

3 Tasks for the day

☐ _____
☐ _____
☐ _____

Gratitude Reflection- What is one thing that you are thankful for today?

_____
_____
_____
_____
_____

Nothing changes if nothing changes, big or small. Just make sure you have vision. If you can't see where you're going, or if a goal or change is too far out of sight, nothing can getdone. Jen Hazzard- Broadalbin NY

December **16**, 20_____

National Chocolate-Covered Anything Day

3 Tasks for the day

❑ _____
❑ _____
❑ _____

Today's Doodle

Gratitude Reflection- What is one thing that you are thankful for today?

_____
_____
_____
_____
_____

December **17**, 20_____

National Maple Syrup Day

3 Tasks for the day

❑ _____
❑ _____
❑ _____

Today's Doodle

Gratitude Reflection- What is one thing that you are thankful for today?

_____
_____
_____
_____
_____

Investing nothing more than time gives us the greatest rewards.
Jessica Rhodes- Tribes Hill

December **18**, *20___*

Today's Doodle

National Twin Day

3 Tasks for the day

- ❏ _____
- ❏ _____
- ❏ _____

Gratitude Reflection- What is one thing that you are thankful for today?

_____
_____
_____
_____
_____

December **19**, *20___*

Today's Doodle

National Hard Candy Day

3 Tasks for the day

- ❏ _____
- ❏ _____
- ❏ _____

Gratitude Reflection- What is one thing that you are thankful for today?

_____
_____
_____
_____
_____

You can tell much about a person's character by how they treat God's "lesser" creatures.
Susan Casler- Glenn NY

December **20**, 20____

National Sangria Day

3 Tasks for the day

❑ _____
❑ _____
❑ _____

Today's Doodle

Gratitude Reflection- What is one thing that you are thankful for today?

_____
_____
_____
_____
_____

December **21**, 20____

National Crossword Puzzle Day

3 Tasks for the day

❑ _____
❑ _____
❑ _____

Today's Doodle

Gratitude Reflection- What is one thing that you are thankful for today?

_____
_____
_____
_____
_____

Once you realize that love, family and friendship are the most important things, everything else seems to fall into place. Melissa Mycek- Town of Perth

December **22**, 20____

National Date Nut Bread Day

3 Tasks for the day

- ❑ _____
- ❑ _____
- ❑ _____

Today's Doodle

Gratitude Reflection- What is one thing that you are thankful for today?

_____
_____
_____
_____
_____

December **23**, 20____

National Pfeffernusse Day

3 Tasks for the day

- ❑ _____
- ❑ _____
- ❑ _____

Today's Doodle

Gratitude Reflection- What is one thing that you are thankful for today?

_____
_____
_____
_____
_____

Most things happen when you don't know where you are going.
Jonathan Blake- Johnstown NY

December **24**, 20____

National Eggnog Day

3 Tasks for the day

☐ _____
☐ _____
☐ _____

Gratitude Reflection- What is one thing that you are thankful for today?

_____
_____
_____
_____
_____

December **25**, 20____

National Pumpkin Pie Day

3 Tasks for the day

☐ _____
☐ _____
☐ _____

Today's Doodle

Gratitude Reflection- What is one thing that you are thankful for today?

_____
_____
_____
_____
_____

As long as you're - always - willing to try you'll never lose- you'll only learn.
Joe Calderone- Broadalbin NY

December **26**, 20____

National Thank-You Note Day

3 Tasks for the day

- ❏ _____
- ❏ _____
- ❏ _____

Today's Doodle

Gratitude Reflection- What is one thing that you are thankful for today?

_____
_____
_____
_____
_____

December **27**, 20____

National Fruitcake Day

3 Tasks for the day

- ❏ _____
- ❏ _____
- ❏ _____

Today's Doodle

Gratitude Reflection- What is one thing that you are thankful for today?

_____
_____
_____
_____
_____

Find your inner star and shine BRIGHT. Danielle Alteri- Amsterdam NY

December **28,** 20____

National Short Film Day

3 Tasks for the day

❑ _____
❑ _____
❑ _____

Gratitude Reflection- What is one thing that you are thankful for today?

_____
_____
_____
_____
_____

December **29,** 20____

Today's Doodle

National Pepper Pot Day

3 Tasks for the day

❑ _____
❑ _____
❑ _____

Gratitude Reflection- What is one thing that you are thankful for today?

_____
_____
_____
_____
_____

Blessings happen for a reason. In fact, everything happens for a reason, be thankful for ALL of those reasons. Faith (Horton) MacLean- Perth NY

December **30**, 20___

National Bacon Day

3 Tasks for the day

- ❑ _____
- ❑ _____
- ❑ _____

Today's Doodle

Gratitude Reflection- What is one thing that you are thankful for today?

_____
_____
_____
_____
_____

December **31**, 20___

National Champagne Day

3 Tasks for the day

- ❑ _____
- ❑ _____
- ❑ _____

Today's Doodle

Gratitude Reflection- What is one thing that you are thankful for today?

_____
_____
_____
_____
_____

Happy Birthday to the love of my life, join me in a cheers to Gabriel!
Happy New Year's Eve!

Many Thanks

There are a few people that I would like to express my thanks to that made this book possible. Without driving forces in our lives we would not shine so bright.

~To my dearest husband & best friend Gabriel for supporting me and my idea. From the first time that I brought it up, he supported and engaged the idea as he knew that this was something near and dear to my heart.

~To all the local (Upstate NY) people out there that contributed quotes! Cheers to you and all that you do to keep us strong and amazing! Thank you to my friend Ali for the proofing!

~To a dear friend whom I have known since my childhood, Chad Leonard. I reached out to Chad to see if he would create my cover for my book as he is an artist. Chad actually told me no! He said, "Heather, I will help you design and make your own."You have a creative side that you have not tapped into. I said ok, and on 12/30/2020 we sat down and started painting. Well, you know the rest. Just close the book & have a look again.

P.S. Never stop improving yourself, everyday is a new opportunity for you to grow and learn new things. Never settle or stand still, keep moving forward in life. Captivate every moment and choose extraordinary measures! Set goals that scare you and take baby steps to achieve them. Much love!